A Recon Marine's Tales

NO JOY

A Genuine Vireo Book | Rare Bird Books

Los Angeles, Calif.

A Recon Marine's Tales of (Self) Destruction

David Rose

THIS IS A GENUINE VIREO BOOK

A Vireo Book | Rare Bird Books
453 South Spring Street, Suite 302
Los Angeles, CA 90013
rarebirdbooks.com

Also available in audio from Talking Book
Originally published as *Spent Shell Casings* from Gatekeeper Press, 2016

Set in Janson
Printed in the United States

10 9 8 7 6 5 4 3 2

Publisher's Cataloging-in-Publication data
Names: Rose, James David, author.
Title: No joy : a recon Marine's tales of (self) destruction / by David Rose
Description: Includes bibliographical references. | Trade Paperback Edition | A
Genuine Vireo Book | New York, NY; Los Angeles, CA: Rare Bird Books, 2017.
Identifiers: ISBN 9781945572494
Subjects: LCSH Rose, James David. | Marines—United States—Biography.
| United States. Marine Corps—Biography. | United States. Marine Corps.
Reconnaissance Battalion, 2nd (1998-)—Personal Narratives. | Fallujah, Battle
of, Fallujah, Iraq, 2004. | Iraq War, 2003-2011—Personal narratives, American.
| Afghan War, 2001—Personal narratives, American. | Post traumatic stress
disorder—Patients—United States—Biography. | Combat—Psychological aspects.
| BISAC BIOGRAPHY & AUTOBIOGRAPHY / Military | BIOGRAPHY &
AUTOBIOGRAPHY / Personal Memoirs
Classification: LCC DS79.766.A1 R67 2017 | DDC 956.7044/30921—dc23

Where are the happy young men
I hung out with in the old days
Who sang so well and spoke so well
So excellent in word and deed?
Some are stiffened in death
And of those there's nothing left
May they find rest in paradise
And God save the ones who remain.

—Francois Villon

CONTENTS

NO JOY: interjection /nō joi/: military term for having attempted to acquire a target that was never found.

~~WARNING ORDER~~
INTRODUCTION

THE US MILITARY'S GROUND combat units contain some of the most prolific degenerates, sociopaths, reprobates, and skilled war fighters the world will ever produce.

The sun setting over a desolate hill, smoke from trash fires hanging, warriors stepped out from their living quarters. Grunts, Rangers, SEALs, Marine Recon, and others wearing plate carriers, drop pouches, and tourniquets, donned their night vision goggles with the hand not holding their rifle. Rolling out of the wire in Humvees, covert local vehicles, or on foot, while others boarded Chinooks and Black Hawks, the tools of foreign policy made their way to hides, houses, hillsides, and mountaintops. "Warriors," "heroes," "modern-day Spartans," and all sorts of other headliners that sell the movie tickets and seduce hundred-pound high schoolers into becoming snipers, those boys set out to observe, to report, to raid, and to kill.

Blasted out of the gun barrel and onto the silver screen, women left in their juices as the next protein shake is mixed, an imposter pulverized at the bar, and a hammer pair shot into the vitals, these best of friends, these sick fucks—teeth-whitening strips inserted as pushups go on for days. Tattoos, steroids, porn, gloating pictures of the dead, precision fire, *pink mist*, and wild nights in whatever town surrounds the training area. Women will scoff and squirm, and men will scoff and bleed. The American warrior: letting the groupies smell the black powder, giving them just a sniff of the chaos as carnage is left in their wake.

The Red, White, and Blue flies before you, yet this time... and for the first time...waves and whips with the wry mania of the best who redden its stripes.

Behold now, alive and lurid, one explanation for why so many millennial men chose to experience war.

1

STONE TOWN AT THE END
OF THE RABBIT HOLE

*Nobody thinks anymore how marvelous it is
that the whole world is diseased.*

—Henry Miller, *Black Spring*

SUMMER 2013

CARVED AND CRAFTED ON a lush green island off the Tanzanian coast, Stone Town, the former slave trade nexus for the Middle East and the African Great Lakes region, sits eternal. The Islamic influence on the island is undeniable, especially for anyone who has spent any real time in the Muslim world. And by "Muslim world," I don't mean any American experience in Dearborn, Michigan, or a mosque next to a McDonalds. Anything American, whether Irish pride in mid-March, or bouts of defense or boasting about a nationality due to a great-grandparent having been born there—the American version is a cheap mimic of the homelands. The home turf is usually a place most Americans wouldn't venture to without a fresh vaccine and a Sandals event coordinator. I'm talking Kuwait, Iraq, Dubai, Afghanistan, and eventually a sliver of East Africa. The Muslim world I patrolled, vacationed, fought, drank, and puked in was of the Eastern Hemisphere species.

Inside an old, bare room, I stand in its mirror. A bow of daylight blasts out from a rip in a moth-eaten curtain. Through the dust and jagged fragments of light, my eyes scan all the tattoos. Punk. Fantasy. Mostly beaten by the sun, and a decade old long before I would look at thirty—coming together like those of a drunken sailor, or a wayward rock and roller maybe. They sit on a thin frame, a frame teased into a semblance of fierceness from readily abandoned lifestyles. Taken as a whole, the mirror shows sort of an early-seventies Iggy Pop without the heroin meets a young Liam Neeson without the talent. A shirt goes over it all and the door flies open.

There is something about stepping onto a dusty street, hearing unseen speakers kick on, and then a man tasked with prayer clearing his throat before the almighty and lengthy "Allaaaaaaaaaaaaaaaaaaah…" There is something about walking down the winding, serpentine alleys, accentuated by the high, white walls, containing large, wooden doors with the Arabic swirls and floral patterns I immediately recognize from the Quran I stole while in the Al Anbar Province. Those strange stares from those sun-beaten faces contrast with their off-white garb, stained with human grease. For a son of the GWOT[1] generation, whether in possession or absent of potent disdain, there is an awkward at-home sensation when immersed in the old world of Islam.

Trying to untie myself from the knot my postgraduate sojourn into analytic philosophy left me in, I had forsaken the London high-rises, efficient plumbing, and society without machetes to cleanse myself in the gritty realism of the third world.

The third world: from a tourist's perspective, you will only get a contorted, angular view of what it's really like. An example follows from my first week on the Dark Continent: stay at a dive

1   Global War on Terror

resort in Nungwi, experience top-of-the-line scuba diving, then enjoy brunch on the boat as malnourished locals scurry to get all the tanks off the vessel and back to the dive locker. Later that evening, watch a tumbling group execute their routine with a good, solid, primitive drumbeat in the background while fully adorned in animal hides, no less campy than a Disney presentation. Tuck off to bed with a good buzz of imported beer—

Wake up in the morning and almost step in a dried pool of blood as large as a manhole cover. This is not a stone's throw from where someone's SPF 50–caked wife sat and Skyped with her sister about "how scenic and lovely and euphoric the place is." Must protect the tourist. Must protect the US dollar and the Euro and the Yuan. The Masai security caught a local man jumping the gate and then, henceforth, beat him to death with their iconic Masai clubs. Having procured one of my own in Dar es Salaam, holding such a club in one's hand makes clear that this culture, whose lineage is bursting at the seams with innumerable tribal conflicts and some of the most extravagant megafauna in the world, has taken the time to perfect their weaponry. The orinka, whose skinny handle is about as long as the average human arm, comes to a sudden bulbous crown. The face of the crown owns a small but significant notch. It was not through a physics class, taught in a land where such practicum is vehemently shunned by the bland and proper, but through trial and error battling man and beast that the Masai learned of the pound-force per square inch, the power of concentrating force into smaller surfaces. Such science was the ultimate reality for the dead intruder.

Life is cheap in many parts of the third world, and the champagne, leaf-blade ceiling fans, and Wi-Fi only distract the naïve tourist long enough to believe that they are not a moment away from being robbed, butchered, or eaten.

After diving off the northern tip, I had pushed south to Stone Town, set up, and punched out. On the west side of the island, at Kendwa Rocks; a sort of party hub where vacationers from various resorts all conglomerate, I walked past a young man talking to an employee at a laundry counter. The thick southern drawl in conjunction with what had to be three "fucks" in one sentence caught my attention. I had come across a few Americans, yes, but it was not common in these parts. Stopping to see who the foul mouth was, I immediately saw green USMC PT[2] shorts and a medium regulation haircut, overgrown by a week or so.

Like the Masons maybe, through the subtleties of word and symbol, we had found one another. In all the great expanse that is Africa, I had somehow stumbled upon a marine. Bud introduced me to the other marines he was with, and I learned that they worked at a nearby US Embassy. On leave and unable to fly back to the States, they swarmed Kendwa Rocks in search of some wine, women, and song. In addition, Bud had flown in a friend from his home state of Alabama. His friend, Bill, was this baby-faced Southerner, somewhat in the realm of a young John Candy, and had never left 'Merika before. Witnessing him converse with the locals, who referred to the USA as "Obama Land," was a lesson in hilarity. He was in pure culture shock, though handling it like a champ. Exposing him to as much *culture* as possible soon became a reoccurring motivator of mine.

The embassy marines asked me what I had done when I was in. I had been a recon marine, to some, a fabled type of grunt.

---

2   Physical training

Infantry: noun \'in-fən-trē\: military personnel trained, armed, and equipped to fight on foot. The colloquialism "grunt" is used interchangeably, in both the US Army and US Marine Corps, for "infantryman."

Special Operations: noun \'spe-shəl ä-pə-'rā-shəns\: groups in militaries trained in unconventional warfare. In the US, popular outfits such as Navy SEALs, Army Rangers, and Army Green Berets fall under this category, as does Marine Recon. The vast majority of Spec Ops are specialized infantry/grunts.

ANSWERING THEM DID WHAT I figured it would do, and the fact that I was from the cowboy days of Iraq made my seat at their table all the cushier. I was quickly given a place among them and palled around with this group for the better part of a week.

After a few nights, the group split in two. The next day we would all rendezvous and take the ferry to the mainland. As one element stayed in the northwest, Bill, Bud, and I traveled south for one last night in Stone Town.

What occurred that night, if put regally, was some strange return to the USMC. I was perhaps begged, or perhaps driven, to show the new generation how fearless and depraved were the alumni of the GWOT's golden age.

We bought beer and sat out on the stone, second-floor balcony that was attached to our room. We were in some ancient building, recently converted into a hostel, and from our height the city was a web of thin power lines, leaning, pointy rooftops, and laundry hung out to dry. The buildings were so close together one couldn't help but contemplate the valiant run-and-jump; the extending porticos and ledges met one another from opposing sides of the cobbled streets.

I had some Ambien on me. I hadn't taken any while diving in the north, or during the safari—but drinking on that balcony, alive with an electric current, realizing that you are there, right then, at that moment. Ambien: it is a mystery of modern medicine how ten milligrams worth of a sleeping pill can cause the extraordinary hallucinations and euphoric states that it does. The first time I took Ambien I was flying from DC to Dubai. A contractor I worked with at the time gave me one, along with some muscle relaxer he failed to identify. Moments and a Miller High Life later, I was transfixed on the swirling waves of blue. Eerily, the TV screens on the back of the headrests in front of me were all showing *Avatar*. The collection of screens danced and swayed, and the chemicals that induced "happiness" flooded my brain as I melted into my seat. The fifteen-hour plane ride was over in a blissful and vivid forty-five minutes.

The VA's[3] refillable answer, I took Ambien on those nights when I would wake up in a sweat and couldn't fall back asleep. The nights when the anthropomorphic nature of my brain made the towel hanging on the bamboo rack a menacing burglar. The nights I was so bored I could cut my feet in the shower just to

---

3   Department of Veteran Affairs

watch the crimson mix with the water and feel alive. Or maybe the nights that I just wanted to talk to the inanimate objects, turned bubbly and full of personality, in whatever room I was occupying.

"I dunno man, my stepmom took some of this shit and ordered three hundred dollars worth of crap from the Home Shopping Network and didn't even remember doin' it," said Bill.

"I dunno, man, there's a shitload of bad shit that I have heard about this shit. People waking up while drivin', err wakin' up with all the knives from the kitchen now in their bed," said Bud.

Once proposed, and reassured of the positive effects, Bill and Bud cautiously accepted their pills.

Out of beer and on the ambiguous shoreline of the pills kicking in, we decided to reemerge out onto the streets. This time we weren't going to wallow with tourists listening to Queen over and over; we were going into the heart of darkness. Our supplies: my MP3 player, several dispersed stacks of Tanzanian currency, Bud's portable speakers, and my Rx bottle of Ambien, just in case.

Heading north, we asked some merchant types what bar the locals go to. Once they were convinced we had no interest in their fish, paintings, or rambutan, several ashy and calloused hands sprouted in unison, pointing in the direction we were already going. The men rattled off a name, but none of us could decipher it, and none of us seemed to care.

Passing some great tree on the inland and a crowded, shallow bay of canoes and fishing boats on the seaside, we saw the town open up a bit. In its grimace was a noisy building, crawling with people like an ant pile stirred with a beer-soaked twig.

The white boys had come into town, as it were. With the recondite properties of the pills broken down to their base forms, flowing through our veins, we entered.

Swinging wide the saloon-style door, the speakers draped around my shoulders and hanging about my armpits played Lynyrd Skynyrd. The setting sun glowed a deep orange all over the nightclubish interior. The fading rays cut through twirling dust and occasionally ended against the few patrons populating the room's bar and edges. I noticed a stairwell leading to an upper deck. We made our way to the bar. Leaning against it were a few young guys who had noticed our entrance and seemed to be amused.

If there is one place that confirms the influence American music has had on the world, it is Africa. These guys at the bar looked like…well, basically, imagine if an alien civilization was in the path of the waves emitted from a year's worth of rap and R&B music videos. If those aliens flew down to the African plains and quickly dressed some cow herder in the regalia of said videos, you would begin to have an understanding of the African take on African American culture.

A mix of eighties-style hi-top fades, opaque sunglasses that would look perfect scowling over the smoking barrels of a sawed-off .410, gaudy fake-gold chains, sweatpants, and Nikes, they welcomed us to sit with them and immediately asked us about New York City.

With Skynyrd turned off and our personal sound system (which was later stolen) placed on the bar, we pounded Ndovu as Fuse ODG was cranked up and the locals began to pour in.

We each took another Ambien and before the fairyland claimed me, I had just enough sense to execute a single action that I credit with saving our asses. I found the biggest guy in the place, alongside some dreadlocked spider who made sure to tell me he was half-Persian.

"Here is twenty USD," I told them. "Follow us around tonight and make sure we don't get robbed, and I will give you another twenty USD back at the hostel."

With our new best friends added to the entourage, we sunk down the rabbit hole.

I remember colors—everywhere—blinking in and out of the dark corners of the crowded nightclub. At one point we were surrounded, the locals pawing at us, fondling the buttons on my shirt. A large man in a black hoodie and a necklace of bones kept coming up to me, getting in my face, and yelling. His hand gestures—leaving trails in their wake—seemed to be some kind of curse. After four or five curses, I didn't turn into a toad, or a snake, or a green card out of that place, which made this club-hopping witch doctor become thoroughly unhinged. As he charged at me, I stood like a pale, laughing statue as my bodyguards intervened and carried him out of the place, kicking and screaming.

Next, the hookers. The guy with dreads was, we came to find out, just the guy we needed. As the sea of dark skin, sweat, and beer suds washed over me, I was weightless. Only after Bill grabbed me by the shoulder and pulled me to the bar's edge did I see our approaching Nubian companions.

Me, Bud, Bill, Big Bodyguard, Little Bodyguard with dreadlocks, and two hookers dressed like New Orleans bar workers in the 1930s wandered throughout a labyrinth of alleys and nooks. The chemical mosh pit in our brains kept hiding our hostel from us. After storming past a beggar to beat on a door that wasn't ours, we sat on a stoop to collect our wits. Our increasingly annoyed attachments were assured "not to worry," and that we'd "find it soon." More marching, and marching more.

By some miracle, one of us noticed a familiar window or intersection of time-beaten stones. Marching past the bewildered clerk, we tromped up the stairs like an invading army. Noise complaints would soon be piling up, as would the steps needed to unleash full pandemonium.

"Bill," I said "where's the damn money?"

"I dunno," Bill said, then laughed, walking into the backroom with one girl, "thought you had it."

"Bud?"

"Don't lookit me, man." And so on.

After a few more blurry deliberations with Bud, I fell back on a most hasty and improvised Plan B. Coming from a life spent surrounded by addicts, I knew firsthand the swaying power of righteous indignation. I blamed the girls—thieves they were.

Turning to the pimp, "What kinda show you runnin' here, buddy?" hands on my hips like a dad at the IHOP, pissed about no refills while his family waits in the Windstar. He got in my face. Lucky for me, Big Bodyguard had disappeared. Maybe that witch doctor's incantation had a delayed effect, I thought, and the cat I saw running in terror as Bud chased it down in hallucinogenic hysteria was actually the big guy. Bud and I could take this little prick and his merry band of working girls.

Bud?

A quick glance over my shoulder—Bud was out cold. Like a corpsman-shooting-the-morphine type of out cold. Behind him was the shut door leading to the room where Bill and his girl had disappeared. In a normal state of mind, I imagine I would have pondered a bit on the bizarre splashes and brief thuds and mumbles coming from Bill's room. I handed the pimp his twenty USD. I was able to scrounge up that much. I thanked him for stopping the cutthroats and pickpockets, and then demanded he take his thieving girls with him. The girl still in the bedroom started screaming in Swahili. Not a moment later the wide-eyed night manager burst in.

With the pimp and prostitute silent and sunk into a corner, the exchange went something like…

"Sir, we have many complaints. You being loud."

"I…I am sorry. Me and my friends here…" I tossed a limp point toward the cornered two. "We were just laughin' about somethin'. We…err…goood nowwww."

Bill's door flew open. It was his girl, and she yelling for assistance. All eyes floated clear over and beyond the comatose body of Bud.

Apparently the overload of pills, foreign beers, Obama talk, and paying for sex was too much for Bill's gastrointestinal system. Naked, half-covered in his own shit, Bill stood with his hands against the wall like he was in a prison reception facility. His back was soaking wet and glistening. Our eyes zeroed in on the bucket the hooker was holding, then we all watched in unison as she tensed her jaw and then gave him another splash. Bill, dripping from the makeshift bath and excrement, turned around and finalized the moment with a big, pearly grin.

The manager and I turned to one another. I couldn't exactly pin his look—expressionless, maybe, with a touch of either solving a riddle or holding in vomit.

The bucket-splasher, learning from her pimp that she wasn't going to be reimbursed for her sanitary services, went absolutely berserk. The bucket flew, and curses in Swahili bounced off the walls like ping-pong balls. The pimp and night manager rushed her, took custody of her, and rolled out of the room like a twelve-limbed monster. I leaped and shut our door.

Bill, still dripping, and I, swaying from the confrontation's heightening effect, gave one another the nod.

We were not done yet.

After Bill cleaned off, we left Bud alone and marched to the nearest cashpoint. Somehow collecting the terrain features we needed, hugging up against the great inland tree and driving onward, we were on our way back to the bar. The streets were entirely different now. It was as if the place was suffering from a puny earthquake. There was a green glow on everything, and I swore the hyena that had run through my camp in the Serengeti had forded the Zanzibar Channel and was now stalking us. Then we were at the face of our destination. The noise coming out of the club pulled at our shirts.

Back inside, we made our way to the top deck. Stumbling against the rooftop bar, I cocked my head to the right. A man wearing big, red-rimmed sunglasses, a red football jersey, baggy leather pants, and poofy red shoes gave me a nod and blew me a kiss. His hair was a series of steps, like something found in the Andes, and his long goatee moved a bit when he smiled. Sitting next to him, a woman was adorned in the same reds and whites. She had straight, silky hair that shined when she leaned toward him to whisper. She looked like a junior varsity Naomi Campbell—one that was smiling at me. There was some class to these two, no war-torn native types. Approaching them was easy, as was getting him to sell her. Bill received her nearby friend, just as cute, but more on the muscular side, if that's your thing, sporting little blue shorts and a white blouse. We shook the guy's hand, and the four of us departed to once again make the perilous trek back.

The night manager was dutifully manning his front desk. His mouth hung open as if seeing the return of problematic ghosts, and from it he let out a sigh as we passed him and ascended the stairs.

Wouldn't you know it, for every cock-blocking additive of this harrowing night, we found ourselves locked out of our room. The best we could do was get to our balcony by way of a common-access door. Once on the balcony, we got on our knees. Staring through a medieval keyhole at Bud, still passed out, Bill and I whispered, "Bud, Budddd…BUD." After twenty minutes or so the key reappeared in Bill's pocket.

Lord only knows what Bill did with his girl. I get the feeling that if people from his hometown learned exactly what he did, and with whom, he would be exiled from the tabernacles for life. Despite an extremely altered mental state, my gear worked like a sixteen-year-old about to get his cherry popped. We made love. Sweet, sweet, financially-exchanged love. She rode me, we kissed. The white silk that served as bug netting for my bed breathed and billowed as we moved. We shared multiple sessions, and the final one…as it was just starting to be revealed exactly how Naomi Campbell she was not…ended just as the sun was rising.

I hadn't been out for more than a few moments before the first call to prayer burst through my window.

"Allaaaaaaaaa—"

The hostel was conveniently right next to a mosque, and the minaret's speakers screamed directly at me and a passed-out hooker.

"—aaaaaaaaaah!!!!" as I shot out of bed, spinning in tight nauseous circles, my eyes clawed at the oil spill carcass that had been lying next to me.

There was some sort of sick circle completed right then, half into my pair of pants. I had first experienced such noisy tradition as a youngster warrior in the farmlands south of Fallujah, then relived it almost ten years later as a weathered nomad turning over every rock. Jeans zipped and pushing into Bud and Bill's room, I saw Bill's girl getting dressed, Bill awake—staring straight up to a slowly moving fan, mouth ajar, and refusing to look at me. Bud, still unconscious, had one of Bill's flung condoms laying smack dab on his forehead.

The prayer ended, the girls departed, and slowly we collected ourselves. I examined the condoms I'd used looking in sheer terror for a rip or hole. Afterward we went down to help ourselves to a much-needed and barely-deserved complimentary breakfast. As we drooped over our eggs and juice, sleep-deprived tourists limped past us in utter disgust.

We had a ferry to catch. We caught it. Bud swore to never take Ambien again. Bill flew home and had a series of bloodwork done, all coming back good. Word spread fast to the other marines what had happened. Sitting at an English pub in Dar es Salaam a couple nights later, I detected an odd energy coming from the group, a sordid royalty gifted. The "old Corps," the Mad Dog Mattis Corps, the field Marine Corps had come to Stone Town. One-man room clears while at war, hedonistic conquests while on leave.

2

ANOMIE ON THE BACK NINE

The Child is father of the Man.

—William Wordsworth

THE '90S

LARGE GROUPS WERE ALWAYS the best. Something about numbers tends to galvanize. If they were too young, it would feel too much akin to schoolyard antics; if they were too old, they would just mumble and call the cops. Ideally, we'd find a few carts filled with blue-collar types mistakenly thinking they were out for an uninterrupted game of golf.

A plant that proliferates in the southeastern United States is the *Dioscorea bulbifera*, or *air potato*. Growing on a vine and ranging in size from a dime to occasional behemoths that look like warty, light-brown grapefruits, the air potato is ideal projectile weaponry.

Kids crouch down in a small ditch. A stepdad's saved army fatigues shield them from poison ivy, bugs, and detection from soon-to-be-furious duffers. Adult-sized camouflage hanging loose over arms and legs, their ears take in the repetitive *ga-gunks* of the cart tires running over the breaks in the concrete trail. Barely audible mumbles snake past the leaves and tree trunks, splits of light show the approaching carts and the Easter-ish golf attire worn by the targets. Arms cocked back, wild, adrenalized smiles wrought from a mixture of excitement and fear, and all waiting for the command. "NOW!" The salvo of noxious weed bulbs flies from the defilade, over the small pond, and their ears wait. The moment of potato flight before potato impact is in many ways the best part. Time seems to slow down. Blood flow surges and feet start to shake, knowing that their duty will be called upon in only a few short moments more. *Thump, thump, thump.* "What the fuck?" "It's fuckin' kids!" *Thump.*

There's no set rule as to what happens next, but usually it's one of two things.

First, the hilarious envelopment attempt by the golfers. With welts and even the rare bloody nose, these taxpayers, PTA attendants, and lords of lawnmowers slam on the breaks, dash madly around the edge of the water hazard, and burst into the wood-line—sometimes as a uniform body, like a small pack of African mongooses, others as multidimensional approaches. Some with clubs, some without, some cursing while others try to catch us in a menacing silence.

Second, and far less frequently, a particularly organized group forms a firing line. Operating under similar rules as the potato barrage, they wait for some sort of command, cock back, then blast Titleists and Slazengers into the woods.

"Nice try, you fat fuck!"

"I'm gonna sell ya these balls back next time ya come out here to suck!"

"Really got a holda that one!"

"You hit me! How could you hit me with a golf ball—I'm just a kid!"

"Hey, don't have a heart attack. We can see that gut from here—bitch!" we yelled, usually rolling in flattened leaves and laughter.

MOVING TO THE NEIGHBORHOOD surrounded by the golf course when I was thirteen, I was put between a rock and a hard place. One of the many middle-American sprawls under the oppressive, maniacally-laughing shadow of Disney World, a suburb called College Park seemed to offer two kinds of teenagers: a washed, upscale type and a drug-saturated hoodlum. I didn't want to be either. I wanted to climb into trees and reread the chapter in *The Hobbit* where Bilbo was in the Mirkwood canopy. I wanted to make dangerous and ill-constructed mounds to jump our bikes over. I wanted to pull pranks, swim the lakes, and do damn near everything both groups grew to shun for their own reasons.

Dabbling in the former group resulted in feeling like some orphan in a Dickens novel, but not the saccharine parts; I mean, the orphan whom the rich look down on, pointing to its dirty hands and placing bets on when winter will claim it. My mom was a public school teacher and my dad a drunkard, a peasant smelling of "cowboy killers" and Budweiser. I was trash with a foul mouth, old shoes, and an occasional propensity for entertaining violent outbursts. I was the one who got reprimanded for bashing a fellow scout's head against a pole at the park, and I was the one who, daringly, hung out with black kids from school, and, even more daringly, racked up wins and losses in my many scraps with them. At best I was tolerated, but the rolling eyes and country-club condescension did not escape me.

However, insertion into the latter group of *hoodlums* was no better. Although I was a bit rough around the edges, I still cared about school and would feel bad about stealing from my parents. In this group, theft was common: money, CDs, whatever their hands could grab when not rolling a blunt or punching out someone who didn't deserve it. The obsession with rap music was both a constant theme as well as a powerful motivator. Ignore the Volvos; we white kids were now in a "hood" and we now miraculously had "enemies" seemingly chosen at random. Pecking orders were established where the most violent, stupid, and belligerent among the crowd were superior to any who gave a fuck about *white boy shit* like grades and saying "please" or "sorry." I was a *bitch*, I would soon learn.

Luckily, able to recruit like-minded dorks and virgins, I took to the sand traps, aprons, and Bermuda grass. The golf course and the entertainment of hurled objects and irate golfers were better than any drug on the street and far more gratifying than some sunny gathering of future lawyers and soccer moms.

The fourteenth fairway was always my favorite place. It's where I walked across to high school for an eternity of groggy mornings, it's where the feud in ninth grade began, it's the area I imagined my dad played on when he was a boy. Small thickets of trees and other vegetation bordered most of the golf course. However, at certain points the vegetation would get inordinately thick, usually around the water hazards. And that was the case with the almighty horseshoe. The fourteenth green, most of the fifteenth fairway, and where the golfers would tee off on the sixteenth were all subject to the same large water hazard and the small forest that had grown around it. It was there that the majority of our assaults took place.

It was also there that I would learn more about military tactics than at any schooling the Marine Corps would later throw in front of me.

Ambush location (Step 1):

We'd reconnoiter positions with the desired proximity: close enough to effectively engage our targets, but far enough to execute a tactical retreat. Cover and especially concealment were fundamental features to be sought. Ideally, terrain dictating, we would locate multiple ambush points using geometry of fire to both confuse the golfers and allow for the most effective potato damage. Whether from a single ambush point or the main point in a multipoint ambush, we'd ensure the golfers' avenues of approach would allow us to monitor their movement. Number of targets, physical size of targets (athletes would often be left alone, unless we had certain logistical advantages), and speed toward the "kill zone" were all observed covertly. The kill zone, where our targets would be engaged, was most opportune when it was a green. They wouldn't be moving much and would be facing inward. A machine-gunner's wet dream: close to one another and totally unaware.

Alternative routes (Step 2):

Once solid ambush locations were determined, we'd plan our egress. Normally we'd plan on individual escape routes. After some time of individual troop movement, we would have a rally point for all to gather. From said rally point, we'd usually return to stealth mode and slip around some terrain feature (e.g., massive thorn bush, driving range, or clubhouse) and make our way into my parents' backyard via an intricate system of loose fence planks and a secret gate behind an apartment Dumpster. If the terrain was familiar, we would have designated routes, as per the thrower, which was second nature due to dozens of live-fire exercises. If the terrain was new, we'd do multiple rehearsals, going over questions that would arise and looking for hidden cypress knots. We found out through painful trial and error the importance of "crawl-walk-run." Once learned, new locations and their subsequent alternate and tertiary escape routes would only be used for the fattest and most lethargic targets.

Ammo caches and fallback positions (Step 3):

Foraging for air potatoes would sometimes predate step one. Rattling vine clusters, climbing trees, or throwing sticks at the massive A-bomb bulbils in the canopy, we'd fill shirts—turned sagging baskets—with our ammunition. Placed along our routes, caches of potatoes would be covered by a lone elephant ear. This became an apparent necessity after a maniacal golfer chased us farther than anticipated. To our good fortune we had accidently left a cluster near our rally point, and one potato the size of a baseball stopped him in his tracks.

Leading from the front (Step 4):

One of the hallmarks of Marine Corps leadership I learned at fourteen. When battering fully-grown men, the potential of a hellacious ass beating didn't escape even the dullest among us. Willingness alone would have gotten us caught. Strategy alone would have never gotten us through the heat of it. It took, as it takes still, both traits to be an effective leader. If it looked like a bad idea, we didn't go through with it. If it looked to be something worthwhile, we not only executed our plan, we did it with tenacity. As the carts approached, or as the putters assembled on the enemy green, I would often look back at them: two brothers from a Pentecostal home so uptight and sheltered that I was nothing short of the Antichrist to their parents. Another, a longtime friend with an arm like a cannon. Two more, timid as the day is long and recruited due to the word of mouth that I would get them up to the snarling face of trouble, yet somehow get everyone out of it in the end.

I would creep to the forward-most edge of the concealment. There were inexplicable moments when our collective gut dropped out of us. Like a small group of VC, or something, we had some serious intentions in those suburban woods. I knew the growing sensation of "fuck it, let's just get the next group" would grow into a mutinous tumor. That was quickly remedied by a smile, nod, and "remember your routes—let's blast these assholes." Uniformly, the salvo of fire would follow the first potato, and morale couldn't have been lowered with a Singapore cane as we ran for our lives amidst the curses of befuddlement and shooting pain.

Some would say the act of throwing things at people is silly, childish, and indicative of a propensity to violate the law and hurt others, and they may be right. But sweating in the woods, skin torn by thorns, dirt in the corners of the eyes, taking risks—we had some courage, and that is more than can be said about most.

———◇———

As is the case, all good things must come to an end. We were, in fact, eventually caught and mightily humiliated; however, we were graciously spared the arrest and the beating. As girls, booze, and concerts took their inevitable precedence over Battlefield: Good Walk Spoiled, the complaints of mysterious bands of potato-chucking kids vanished altogether. Scrapes and cuts on my limbs vanished as well, in their place came body hair and tattoos. When the time came that I donned a camouflage uniform once more, golfers teed off, chipped, and drank in peace.

3

NEVER SHALL I FORGET

FALL 2003

I HAD KICKED, SCREAMED, and likely violated every form of command structure and military courtesy in existence. As a result, I was allowed to take the Marine Recon screening. This was most likely to shut me up, as well as to stoke the furnaces for the years of teasing and torment that would follow my humiliating failure.

I think I slept an hour the night before, then got up at some god-awful time to drive from main side to Courthouse Bay to meet a few other fleet guys waiting on the white bus from SOI[4]. It was time, and I was ready.

As usual, before any great undertaking, I had to take a nerve-rattled shit, this time in a cluster of trees. After sacrificing a sock, the screening began and at the end, upon passing, my bare foot was welcomingly bloody.

The day I officially arrived at 2nd Reconnaissance Battalion, I was handed some gear and a paper copy of the Recon Creed, was given a barracks room, and immediately slinked away into its closet. With my head in my hands, a wave of "be careful what you wish for" immersed me.

I had fought so hard to get to that moment. I was there and took a cynic's inventory of my skills and conditioning, evaluating whether I had prepared enough or had brought a knife to a gunfight.

I knew that if I failed I was damned to go back to the artillery regiment—for me at least, a fate worse than death. Giving credit where credit is due, there were solid marines and professionals scantily peppering the ranks. In addition, many artillery marines in the GWOT era would end up occupying an infantry-centric role, some of whom wouldn't see a single howitzer in country and got into as many gunfights as numerous infantry members. However, this does not blind the eye to the SNCOs[5] who could barely speak the English language, likely destined to work at Home Depot upon their reluctant retirement from the holy fucking Marine Corps— desk clerks who never saw a bush past the hedgerow entrance to base housing, and those pitifully unfit trying to exude the maxim of the Marine Corps warrior culture and killer instinct. Frankly, as an aggregate, it was a waste of government money, and I spent most of my days cutting grass, picking up trash, filling up space at change-of-command ceremonies, and wishing possibly the most common wish of all time: that I'd had a more ethical recruiter

With my head in one hand and the Creed in the other, I scanned it, tracing all the outlines of harshly typed words. Memorizing those words was the first thing I had any real power over—the first step in a great vetting and then emergence into a new MOS[6], a new unit, a new life.

What is the Recon Creed? Some say it was stolen from the Army Rangers, then heavily modified. It's a good way to stir up a mug-draining debate, often proprietary and occasionally tempestuous. I never cared where it came from. No matter the literary origin, it

---

5   Staff non-commissioned officers; E-6 to E-9
6   Military occupation specialty; fancy term for someone's job

doesn't alter the sweat either group pours out or hold any weight on the ways they forcibly alter the world around them.

The Creed consists of five paragraphs, each starting with the letters that spell RECON. The first paragraph starts with *R*, the second with *E*, and so on. Within these five paragraphs is purportedly our community ethos. A decade removed, one can see the generalities of "not giving up" as qualities seen in the Army Rangers—or hell, boot camp, maybe even the Cub Scouts. In fact, many of the principles mentioned don't really distinguish Marine Recon from much of anyone. That is, until you put the fat to the fire. A saying such as "never quit" means something entirely different to a group of young Ropes who knocked out a seven-mile log run on no sleep, or low-crawled in the sugar sand on Onslow for a quarter mile, followed by a 1,500-meter fin out past the breakers and back prior to the Bulls coming out to feed. The Recon Creed, printed and in the hand of a recon hopeful, was a map, manifesto, guidebook, and bible.

The next day, morning PT began—and I do mean morning. There is an odd snap and lick that you feel when running around certain places in Camp Lejeune in the late fall. Stinging snot makes its way down out of the maple and pine, hitting your skin right about the time the cold sets into your lungs. An intense run through bush, brush, and a few skinny trails later, we were standing in a formation on Ellis Field.

"You," said an instructor.

"Yes, Sergeant!" Chris yelled. I'd met Chris the night prior. He'd stormed into my room, burped, announced he was to be called "Bullet," and then stumbled out.

"First paragraph."

Bullet began, "Realizing it is my choice and my choice alone I—"

One done. Another straight-face then picked out of the pack by the fixed-eyed RIP[7] cadre. "Second paragraph." A bit of a pause, an initial stutter, and then the next paragraph was recited.

How I hoped they wouldn't pick me. My palms, clammed and sweaty, tickled at their center. I was brand new to the RIP platoon. These guys had just returned from Fort AP Hill where they had gotten their nuts crushed. This was a unified group, tightened by the fraternity that suffering brings, and I knew I had to earn a place among them, somehow. I was also nervous because I had a growing feeling that one of the instructors was going to eye me out of the group so I could ingloriously fuck up the lines I'd tried so hard to memorize the night before. Who knew if one of the cadre was in a particularly bad mood; I could smell the artillery chow hall from there.

Third paragraph over, recited perfectly, and now on to the fourth. The guy right in front of me got summoned for this one, and boy was he doing lousy. Through the forest of lean bodies in green, I could see the disdain on one instructor's face, all the more illuminated as he came closer to the stutterer, eyeing me while he approached. Our selected orator spit up the last portion, apparently just well enough to pass.

It was time for the final paragraph. They asked for volunteers. Volunteers? Volun—go-fuck-yourself—teers? They always called someone out of the group, but not this last one.

"None of you motherfuckers know the whole thing?"

I found that I had raised my hand, barely.

I felt the way a deer must feel the moment its worst fear is confirmed and it sees the predator make its first step in its direction. Eyes fixed on me. "Go," he said with a slightly menacing nod, partly riddled with a look of *I have no clue who the fuck this guy is.*

---

7   Reconnaissance Indoctrination Platoon

"Never shall I forget the principles I accepted to become a Recon Marine: Honor, Perseverance, Spirit, and Heart. A Recon Marine can speak without saying a word and achieve what others can only imagine." I hid a monstrous gulp—then waited.

"...How long have you been here?" asked the instructor.

"Uh...three days, Corporal."

Extending his neck forward and cocking his chin up. "This guy's been here three days and knows the entire thing. How come you fucks don't?"

I had apparently gotten it right. It was here, at this exact moment, that I first learned of a ritual deeply ingrained into the world of Marine Recon.

"Everyone else, twenty-five and five," demanded the instructor. I felt awkward and naked and alone as the rest of the RIP platoon dropped to the pushup position, a simple, often-executed exercise that served as a reminder for why we were there. Twenty-five pushups followed by a moment of stillness, then five more pushups, these somehow qualitatively different than the rest. Whether on a pool deck, a LZ[8], a beach, or Ellis Field, the twenty-sixth through twenty-ninth pushup would all end with a unified "Wannabe!" and conclude at the thirtieth with "Wannabe Recon!"

With a full stomach, a good night's rest, and muscles that aren't baying like the hounds of hell, the event is rather tame. However, capping off a few rainy, miserable days in the field, eaten alive by bugs and chased by an alligator, ducking under lightning storms and carrying an oppressive load on your back over every stump, log, and bramble...the event is something quite different.

In my life prior, I had always been surrounded by the cult of the obliged—kids forced to play Little League, students who held

---

8   Landing zone

no interest in learning, employees in jobs they hated, and spouses in marriages they despised. Yet suddenly, by merely signing a few pieces of paper and forgoing some personal freedoms that weren't doing anything for me anyways—then just taking some pain—I found myself embedded in a living body of pure determination. I was among people who wanted something as much as life itself, and the word *wannabe* was blasted out of voice boxes with the intensity of a high-speed collision, and done so many more times.

As they rose in unison, wiping the wet blades of grass off the palms of their hands, I was squirming in my running shoes. They were going to be mad at me for making them push. But rather, I was applauded for learning it so fast. Sure, there were some teases later, some good-humored threats and locker-room antics, but their collective reaction, the chorus from pushups twenty-six to thirty, was indicative of the caliber of man I was to be working with in the very deadly near future.

4

ATTACK OF THE
TREASURE TROLLS

Well-intentioned souls now offer me their sympathy and tell me how
horrible it must have been. The fact is, it was fun.

—R. B. Anderson, *Parting Shot: Vietnam was Fun(?)*

FALL 2004

TRITON 2[9] WAS PLACING a detachment for a daylong OP[10]. Our vehicles were staged on a notorious road in the Zaidon[11]. River Road, named for running along the northern shore of the Euphrates, was so littered with IEDs[12] that, for a point in time, a platoon would get hit up to four times in a single day.

In the driver's seat of the lead Humvee, I sat and watched a team make their way to the river's edge. Suddenly, a call came out on the battalion net. A platoon from another company, Plague 1, was being ambushed and we were the closest platoon to the fight. As the word was being disseminated now on our platoon frequency, my blood was pumping like a caged animal about to be freed on taunting, passing prey.

---

9   Also "A2"; my platoon in Iraq
10   Observation post
11   A rural area, south of the city of Fallujah, in the Al Anbar Province of Iraq
12   Improvised explosive devices

This was going to be my first firefight and I couldn't get there soon enough. More than just "getting some," I had close friends in Plague 1. They were in trouble and fighting to potentially save their lives was the only thing that held priority over the need to kill someone.

Watching the guys heading for the OP was a bad Benny Hill skit. They'd quickly shed their gear, put it back on, then off, then on again. Apparently there was confusion as to whether they were going to assist in Plague 1's support or keep on with the mission. The decision came over the radio for them. They ran back to their Humvee right as I was given the word to start our convoy toward the bullets.

Fishtails, skids, and parting herds of goats with impunity, my Humvee led the way. It wasn't long before we could see smoke. It was thick, black, and appeared to be coming from a single source.

Plague 1 was patrolling an area in the Zaidon where a large bridge was being built. My platoon had been all over that exact area just a few days prior uncovering numerous weapons caches. One thing I recall was the land mines, Italian I believe, and how terrified I was handling munitions and explosives I wasn't familiar with. On this day, Plague 1 had driven right into a massive ambush. Numbers were reported to us as approximately 120. Plague 1 was twenty-five men, at most. Truth be told, I have no clue how the hell the number 120 was formulated, but higher Intel stuck with that number, and so it was written.

As we neared from our elevated position, I saw all the black smoke coming from a lone Humvee. It was on a small dirt road, and engulfed in fire. We rolled up to meet a few of Plague 1's lead Humvees that were crawling toward us. As the one Humvee raged in flames, the rest, sturdy like beetles, were growling onto the hardball[13].

Plague 1 let out sporadic volleys of fire from their crew-served weapons. Enemy! As hard as I tried, however, I couldn't see what they were shooting at. All I could see were Americans.

Under the booming of the gun trucks, marines on foot, some bandaged and all draped in random weaponry, made their way to the berm. It was apparent that they were at least a partial group of the blazing vehicle's former occupants. I recognized two of them immediately.

We unloaded out of our Humvees like they too were on fire. Guns up and members thickening, we collectively scanned toward a massive, grown-over berm that ran parallel to the road we were on. Word was making its way onto our radios that the main body of the ambush came from the berm. I tried to listen more. Voices crackled out from the handset. My attention was soon pulled, however, to the one-man freak-out occurring to my left.

Plague 1's platoon sergeant, a man disliked by most, had been one of those in the destroyed vehicle. Losing his primary weapon to the flames, he had an M40 sniper rifle strapped behind his back like a quiver and sported a cigar in his mouth. He would periodically remove the cigar and yell at the Plague 1 platoon commander: "They are enveloping us from the north!" or "This is fucked up, sir!" and a few other one-liners that frantically questioned our two-platoon action of staying put. Things almost got right interesting when he gave up on his superior and moved to one of his team leaders. This team leader was an operator from the previous Recon unit that we'd relieved. He'd stayed behind to work with us and would later win fame for killing an Iraqi man with a knife. The cigar-wielding E-6[14] was sort of choking this

13   Slang term for paved roads
14   Staff sergeant. Of the enlisted rank structure, working up from E-1 to E-9

team leader, losing it, along with any remaining respect his men had for him. Some people in the Corps just have it rough, I guess.

My own team leader had banged that platoon sergeant's cousin's wife, and a late-night encounter in a pool hall, before we deployed almost relit that powder keg before my very eyes.

Word soon came to our platoon that Plague 1 was nearly out of crew-served ammo. Random Triton 2 members, along with our combat engineer attachments, unstrapped ammo cans of 7.62, MK-19[15], and .50-cal[16] and ran them to the smoking weapon systems. Toward me came one of our engineers, bereft of his metal detector for once and laden with two cans of MK-19. He was panting, smiling, and didn't skip a beat when I playfully kicked him in the ass as he passed me. He would be dead a few days later, blown forty feet into the air like a rag doll. He expressed to a comrade just prior to that day that *this* day, fighting alongside Recon, was the most fun he ever had in his short, happy life.

My team was in full swing with Dez, a powerlifting health freak who grew up near Amish country, to my immediate left. My team leader shoved our most junior man out of the turret and was unloading a belt of .50-cal tracers into a two-story house across the river. The brilliant pop of light against the walls, followed by the delayed *thwack* of the impact. Yet not everything was so brilliant. For one, Dez and I took it upon ourselves to confront this alleged "envelopment from the north." However, we didn't see the raiding party of mujahedeen. We did see faint movement in ditches.

They were crawling toward us.

---

15   Pronounced "Mark 19": belt-fed, blowback-operated, air-cooled, crew-served, fully automatic grenade launcher
16   M2 machine gun: crew-served, air-cooled, belt-fed machine gun firing .50-caliber BMG cartridge

White ribbons of movement, AK-47-wielding men in man-dresses were advancing on their bellies—and they were shot. The next day, during a comprehensive BDA[17], we learned a bit more about our enemy. It was a few cows, apparently trying to avoid their obscure cow death, and in vain.

Having stopped all movement from the north, and semi-convinced that we had just "got some," we turned around just in time to watch Chase's SAW[18] drum detach from the weapon. Chase was a country boy, modest and never one to have a quick temper, but with his SAWs ammo belt extending down to his boots with a furious *veeeeep* sound, his "oh shit, goddamn it" in a thick southern drawl forced the rest of us into a burst of laughter.

As Chase fought with his unruly SAW drum, over and over again, going into an ever-increasing downward spiral of curses and mumbles, the rest of my team positioned southward, scanning for enemy movement. In the spray of Chase's frustration, our most junior operator, freshly kicked out of his turret, wasn't about to miss out on the action. He was a red-faced drunkard from some dearly-missed, snowy suburb. He'd put his M4 on full auto. A gleaming stream of gold flew from the ejection port as he conducted several speed reloads.

In league with his ferocious expenditure of ammunition, the truck next to us, possibly the most bizarre team in the entirety of Marine Recon, was going apeshit.

A four-man team, three of whom looked like frat boys who would make the nine o'clock news for a prescription drug ring and a keg-fueled case of date rape. The fourth man, the team leader, was a squatty, bald man, reminiscent of a drunken Russian built from years of chopping logs in the permafrost. At first, appearing

17   Battle damage assessment
18   M249 squad automatic weapon: belt-fed light machine gun that fires the 5.56 x 45–millimeter NATO cartridge

gross and overweight, with severely outdated ARS[19] deuce gear squeezed against him, after a single gym exploit, one would know his body, while it would have been burned and dismembered before ever being displayed on a recruiting poster, actually housed an immense strength.

His three subordinates, all with hair so grossly out of regulation it would give a garrison commando a coronary, were blasting away in the direction of the enemy berm. One was on a mounted M240G[20], and the other two on a knee, bent forward, hugging their M4s into them. Watching them all, it became apparent they were fighting an enemy that somehow continued to elude me.

Their team leader must have shared my reality. "Cease fire! Ceeeease fiiire!" he yelled, frantically flapping his arms like a robust chicken. But it was no use, the three were on some communal rampage. Their hair, maybe as excited by the melee as that of static electricity, was standing up and swaying in the wind. Looking like treasure trolls, they tore the air, firing at anything and everything, unleashing some crazed frustration that had been building since stepping foot in Iraq—but I would reckon had existed long before.

I stood there. Sheer amazement. But was taken quickly out of low-grade hypnosis when an Apache's thirty-millimeter casing bounced off the top of my helmet. Two Apaches, having come swiftly from the north, were now executing *gun runs*, one following the other. From the ground view, the violent, low-altitude maneuvers were an amazing thing to witness. The deliberate, quick, repetitive bursts of their M230 chain guns hummed in the air. As they flew in low at times, showering our

---

19   Amphibious Reconnaissance School
20   Belt-fed, gas-operated medium machine gun that fires the 7.62×51–millimeter NATO cartridge

convoy in shells, one could see the Apaches rock and wobble as last-minute adjustments were made for a retreating enemy they could actually see.

Word came from the birds that most of the remaining enemy were fleeing into the river, while a diehard remnant laid dispersed on the other side of the berm, as well as in an overgrown field between us and it.

After several more runs, the Apaches departed. Next, the field artillery.

Coming in with the occasional *whoo-whoo-whoop* overhead, followed by the dirt-throwing concussion of impact, volleys of artillery munitions rained down from the howitzers in Camp Fallujah.

I was terrified beyond belief. Having been former artillery myself, I could just imagine some degenerate with a horseshoe haircut, dreaming of the underage beer joints or jack-shacks in Lawton. Doing so while calculating death's rain in proximity of my naked location. And they kept coming.

Wow…so we are going to include everyone, I thought, as it became increasingly suspicious that Higher's thrilled and understandable opportunity to check every box they could was, in fact, occurring.

> Nine line; check. Call for fire; check. Let's get those goddamn Small Craft faggots out there and clean house! We gotta mortar platoon anywhere in the area? And get the FAC on the horn about some fixed wing.

The last shell landed, the last rifle fire spat at the distant berm, and both platoons were saddled up. No one on our side died, and later the Plague 1 boys told us of the encounters prior to our arrival. Apparently seeing our trucks was too much for Haj, but before we came swooping in for the action, some intense one-on-

ones transpired, including Iraq's answer to the high-noon duel, SAW versus RPG[21].

My first firefight, if it can be called that, was an interior mixture of exhilaration, confusion, and hilarity. The thirty-millimeter casing that hit my head, which would have made a great double shot glass, would later be confiscated by US Customs. Triton 2, or at least members of it, laughably went berserk at the first opportunity to do so. The blatant disregard for ammo conservation, or even positive identification for that matter, was indicative of some truer intentions than passing out MREs[22] or securing elections.

21　　Rocket-propelled grenade: common weapon of enemy in both Iraq and Afghanistan
22　　Meals ready to eat

5

TONY PREACHING IN
MY DREAMS

SPRING 2011

BACK IN FLORIDA; A solid break in the median, no guard rail, and not a cop in sight, I quickly but carefully pull an illegal U-turn. My freshly hired lawyers want me in their office, wanting to cache my truck and likely myself along with it. With only a couple of hours to get there, I fight the typical vehicular congestion and try to avoid main thoroughfares. Most nerve-racking of all, they need crucial paperwork that is at my house, a place that is likely being watched. Just a few years prior, I was a cop myself; now I'm on the run.

> Still jet-lagged from the Kabul flight, an insane and rock-bottom night, accused of and involving: a bullet through a TV screen, white Russians, a series of incendiary texts, three sliced tires, and a dead chicken, a caprice of mind-shattering random action resulted in nothing short of a man hunt.

Leaving my house, the needed paperwork strewn about the passenger floorboard, I creep out of the subdivision and toward the law offices. Undetected, I become a bit more galvanized as I make my way onto a main road. "Band on the Run" plays in my truck's tired sound system; I keep hearing "man on the run." I visualize, as best I can, some perspective of my situation, just this time not desperate, but noble—a figure from the Wild West.

Grandiosity got to me, some coping mechanism for sure; in years I would be praised for my audacity and never-say-die perseverance, owned by no master but my renegade heart.

Making my way back to the familiar, I cut right through the same exact streets I myself had once policed. The strange days that followed Recon. I see the gas station where the lady was carjacked, pass where that Mexican guy was stabbed to death outside the pawnshop, and the places I would nod off at 4:00 a.m. while listening to radical AM radio DJ mutants stuffed into only the most obscure hours. I pass the road that leads to the subdivision where a filming of animal porn went bad, resulting in the death of a girl, cyanotic and pumped full of pit bull semen. I make it, in cliché fashion, just over the "county line." Traffic slows to a crawl and then it happens: a swarm of unmarked law enforcement vehicles box me in at a red light. I watch their guns and badges draw down on me.

<hr />

YEARS AFTER I RETURNED to the civilian world, I found myself once again fighting for my life. This time, however, it was not in the prone, like a flounder, trying to avoid a salvo of AK-47s, nor was it trying to avoid mortar impacts while returning to a patrol base. It was arguably the biggest legal shit storm since the O.J. trial, and I would spend almost a year and half scratching a GPS anklet the way a recalcitrant dog battles it out with an E-collar.

Just prior to this low-grade hell of attending docket soundings, dodging the scowls of a rabid and personally invested prosecutor, losing my house, my job, the ability to stay out past midnight and/or swim in a fucking pool, I had done what many former infantry and special operations boys of the GWOT generation did: contracted for the big bucks. I'd left Recon, left civilian law enforcement, and opted the third armed go-round for money to be the top priority. One thing uniformly experienced by contractors, other than the money, is the righteous mixing of various services. Two 4th ID[23] guys, an Army Ranger, a grunt from 1st Battalion/ 5th Marines, and three recondos are now on the same team, usually combing their glorious beards in a black SUV or playing *Angry Birds* in a Bearcat. It's a great way to meet like-minded dudes, and the war stories were a thing that rarely, if ever, ceased.

That was over.

Tossing and turning in my bed one night, refitted in my old room at my parents' house, packed tightly between the contents of the home I had just lost, I had the most profound of dreams.

It was not uncommon in those days to have vivid head trips. One in particular was when I was in a tiny bar, so dank and gritty that the noon day could have been mistaken for midnight. I was being interrogated by some vulture of a woman with Reagan-era shoulder pads in her business coat, hair like a schoolmarm, spitting her poison my way while poking her long, bony finger into my chest. Her entourage was a goon squad of middle-aged men, also in business attire. Their faces were quintessential of Shakespearean heat, elevating from irritated to contemptuous and finally to violent. Prior to being ripped to shreds by the system manifest, I bolted out the saloon door. Wolves were on my heels, spilling out from the black mass that I knew to be woods across the street from the bar. In front of me was a lone streetlight, shining down on a solitary object: the first Harley Davidson I had

---

23   Infantry division

ever owned. It was my freedom, in its entirety. Jumping onto the seat, gripping the bars, and setting its circulatory system ablaze, I got low in the saddle. As I sped off, I slowly awoke and didn't move for quite some time after.

This night, as I tossed about, I contemplated the dark tides that assisted in my swift and maniacal downfall. Among others, two out of my three character references on a former security clearance were gone: one dead, one good as dead.

At some point I fell asleep.

I was in a room. There were dark blue walls and the faint wisps of smoke that inexplicably occupied many of my dreams. I was a soul at zero, a complete victim of the world. Helpless. Dumb. Feeble. I admitted it to myself, I was a failure, and worse than losing friends, trust, or face was the complete loss of controlling my own destiny. Unable to weep, I lay still for a while.

Something shifted. Due to some force I could not identify, I slowly arose from a fetal position to come to my knees, seeing the figures that were now in front of me.

If one could mesh a football locker room with the pulpit of a holy roller, this was surely it. Tony, a tall, lanky, black army guy I had met in Texas in 2010 and whom I worked with on random occasions in Kabul, was barely able to stand on one leg. Writhing and undulating as if he were the leader of an encampment of Hard Shell Baptists going over the juicy sections of the good book, he was a man on a mission. Looking dead into my eyes, occasionally clasping his hands together, soon returning to their wild flailing, he emitted words too perfect to remember in the land of the awoken.

Behind him was a seated picket line of men I recognized from the Recon days. The one I remembered the most vividly was a guy who I had gone through RIP and ARS with, and we ended up being in cells next to one another in SERE[24]. All of these seated men stared at me, not in judgment, but in something else. Necks stiff, shoulders rolled forward, arms hung slightly in front of them, they nodded as Tony preached the truth.

In my most drastic times of need and loneliness, it was the idea and remembrance of my brothers-in-arms that gave me strength. Not family, not clinging to some ancient dogma, but the men who knew the savage things that I knew, that saw me, as I saw them, blossom into our own time and place, beautifully and fierce.

Tony smiled; his warrior-choir nodded in agreement. I awoke. Not too long after, a recon brother came to help save my life for the second time. The only difference between the turret with a MK-19 and the courtroom witness stand was that the celebratory chicken dinner afterward wasn't out of an MRE.

---

24   Survival Evasion Resistance Escape

6

BOOT NIGHT

W E, A MERRY GROUP of three, decided that this Friday night was to be special. Having heard the rumors that recon boys out in Cali had occasionally dressed like SOI students and gone out into town to party, we decided to bring this upon Jacksonville, North Carolina.

Boot: noun \'büt\: a pejorative term indicating someone new to the military. Emphasizing both close chronological proximity to graduation from boot camp, as well as the figuratively lowly place among both the enlisted and officer communities.

Donning the boot attire meant we needed to find the right men for the wardrobe collection. Personally, I didn't own any "OORAH, it's a Marine thing" T-shirts, or a beat-me-up jacket with a massive EGA[25] on the back. We had to somehow find a person in recon barracks who actually owned the clothing necessary to pull off this histrionic caper. We knew immediately who to turn to.

In every ground-pounding unit that has ever existed, it seems there is some bizarre personality spliced into the ranks. Some "how the fuck" completely slamming back to the ground any grandiose fantasy that your unit is all Hollywood badass. It is

---

25   Eagle Globe and Anchor: iconic symbol of the Marine Corps

almost certain that when Genghis sent Jebe and his two tumen to capture Kuchlug, during the final moment of Kuchlug's freedom, some runt-of-the-litter, squirrelly Mongol was on the crest of the hunting party; and that even during the exhilaration of capture, a few Mongols writhed at the irksome, unintimidating appearance of their comrade.

Rapping on their barracks door, they answered, glasses first. Putting the *Dance Dance Revolution* pad away, they took us to their closets, where in no time we had an armful of scarlet and gold.

Now I must admit, I dressed the most conservative of the three. In a white USMC shirt with some cliché cartoon on the back of rifles, fantastic creatures, and scary animals, I also wore my MCMAP[26] tan belt and some desert boots (with dog tag inserted, of course). Isaac and Derrick, however, were to be the Tweedledee and Tweedledum of what was sure to be a most magnificent "libo[27] incident."

Isaac hailed from the rust belt. With his blue eyes, boyish face, and body like a statue, running next to him on the beach was humbling only second to contrasting my frequent cynicism against his unbreakable good attitude. Derrick, from Chicago, left Recon a legend to some, a cancer to others. Not even slightly affected by cliché Marine Corps attitudes, Derrick proudly maintained the most out-of-regulation Malibu haircut on the entire East Coast. But despite a facade of unprofessionalism, he contained an incredible aptitude and physical ability, and while he blatantly challenged dubious Marine Corps tenets, his covert love for the job and community would peer out from time to time, usually when no one was looking.

Both with white undershirts, they wore red sleeveless Marine shirts, one stating "Marines" in white and the other stamped

26   Marine Corps Martial Arts Program
27   "Liberty"; time off

"USMC" in gold. Outdoing my tan belt, they went with our more formal web belt. Moving down, they bloused their jeans into their desert boots. Derrick, as per SOP[28], added a few more trinkets. With his dog tags hung out on his chest, cammie paint still under his eyes, like mascara, from the sniper school he was in the process of completing, and an ammo pouch on his hip, we were now geared up, outfitted, and in the proper uniforms.

Next, the pregame. When I was in artillery, I learned of a game called Power Hour. A CD with sixty songs, all only lasting their first minute before bleeding into the next, necessarily exists at the core of this game. Upon the transition from song to song, the players take a shot of beer. It is the type of game where there are no winners or losers per se, just those who finish and those who don't. Having played it a few times, I learned it was common to see first-timers scoff at how easy the game is during the first quarter or so—taking double shots or something. But, Power Hour, of any drinking game to ever be played, has a way of sneaking up on you. Right around the fortieth minute it crosses everyone's mind: "Hey, some asshole made this CD so the songs get shorter and shorter!" For the last ten minutes, you seem to be taking a shot moments after the one before.

And this was the fate of our pregame. We had sucked a few others into my barracks room, turned on the music, and started tearing into the twelve-packs. What was exactly an hour later, we spewed out and onto the lawn of BB 148. I grabbed our standard bottle of Jägermeister. Derrick and Isaac were standing in the uniform of the day, arguing with one of our more melancholy recon brothers. This almost permanent buzzkill had brought some friends from his hometown to enjoy our company. Derrick and Isaac had tasked themselves with figuring out why the fuck

---

28   Standard operating procedure

they weren't immediately coming out with us; then later came up with some makeshift, slightly-staggering comm plan: "OK, dude, you guys go now, and when we are ready we will meet you down there. Everyone got a phone? Good—"

Meanwhile my focus turned to a peculiar, bipedal monstrosity that was slumped over against the front wall of our barracks. This thing, clothed in blue jeans and placed accordingly to their ergonometric instructions, looked human enough. Brown, pinkish skin over gut, chest, and back—all features starting to ring a bell. This thing reared its head up, exposing its drink-ravaged face. Then he threw up. Big-time. It was Dirt, a guy from our Bravo Company. He had sat in on the Power Hour game, disregarded the rules, and paid the price. Now, Dirt was on all fours, projectile vomiting onto the grass. Despite the spectacle of Dirt, the thing that stuck out more was actually the two random guys, just standing there, behind him. For years Derrick and I debated who the hell those two actually were. New joins? Family members of some marine not cut loose on libo yet? A couple of the CIA's SAD[29] guys, getting precise intel regarding the American Marine Corps' garrison habits, with specific emphasis on returning Victor units several months back to the retrograde of the garrison growl?

"—Good, let's get the fuck out of here!"

Anyway, Dirt was done. The original three, the merry band of brothers, we called for a taxi-van. We hopped in and said we wanted to go somewhere our outfits wouldn't be appreciated. The three-hundred-pound behemoth driver, a woman who once offered to suck my dick for twenty dollars, got a gleam in her eye. The sliding door shut, that fat hand ripping the shifter out of "P" and throwing it back into "D"…We all knew where we were going.

---

29   Special Activities Division

Not far off SR-17 sat the bar. We were in the American Southeast, and in a military town no less. It was all too easy finding a shitbox that had chew stains on the wooden planks, hyper-patriotic insignia flying about, some tonk twangin' good and loud, and a few good ol' boy marines ready to stomp some ass. Hell, even the civilians may have been ready to kick in a throat if someone—some inexplicably stupid, rude motherfucker—disrupted the sanctity of their watering hole. And God save the one who stole the attention of the woman who should've been lavishly stroking the brim of their cowboy hat.

I paid the cab fare. Isaac started giggling. Derrick marched straight for the front door. The first "hell nahh" was soon followed by a second. Then the "you gotta be shittin' me!" followed by waves of half-confused laughter and an audible ruckus resembling a disturbed chicken coop. By the time Isaac and I had sifted through his wake and gotten inside, Derrick was standing in the entrance, hands on hips, proud, like something you would see in the Louvre. Then he turned and flashed an unmistakable "allllll right, mutha-fuckers, it's on" smile.

The reactions were incendiary at points, comical at others. Sad, drunk faces at the bar, cowboy hats atop such, slurring their disdain. It was at these moments that Derrick would snap to the POA[30] and give the slowest, most "fuck you" salute in the world. Ike and I could do nothing but cheer him on, laugh, and occasionally see if a crowd was gathering anywhere to try and take us out.

Derrick took off to find girls and conveniently had the ammo pouch secured to his waist, allowing him to peruse the dance floor with a full Bud Light in tow. I scanned the bar. One guy was still sunk in his sad rage, slowly mortaring his stare from Derrick to Ike and me. Only suicidal civilians or manically disrespectful

---

30   Position of attention

boots would waltz in—one giving him a salute, then running off
to find pussy. Ike and I could only help by yelling across the bar,
"What?!" "What, pussy?!"

At about an hour in, still not a single punch had been thrown.
This was right around the time a long-standing theory of mine
originated, one that I've been nurturing for many years since.
It has only been solidified by traveling to the world's blacklists:
Look sick enough and even the predators leave you alone. We
behaved so flamboyantly, so campy, those who most certainly
had been contemplating killing us had to consider the legitimate
possibility they'd very well get the shit kicked out of them by a
bunch of clowns.

At some point our late-party made it. Checking the Nextel
clipped to his web belt, Ike informed us of their arrival. The place
had packed itself like a draft-sponsored slaughter house, so we
slipped past chuckles and mean-mugs to get out the front door.
Outside somehow wasn't much better. It almost looked like the
waning stages of some crime scene: yellow "caution" tape rolled
up and blood stains hosed to obscurity, all that is left is the gaggle
of milling onlookers. Our late-party was yet to be identified, so
we decided to hang out and continue our thespianic assault on
all in eyeshot.

Filing out of a van, similar to the one that had brought us, a
genuine group of boots emerged. The Real Motivators. Standing
in a makeshift formation no less, they had donned as much regalia
as we had. There was an odd, prolonged exchange of glances
between our groups.

"Who is the father of Marine Corps aviation?" I lobbed at them.

"A. A. Cunningham," answered their leader. They were
allowed to pass, and as I watched them march into the bar,

I wondered if they'd feel the mounting blowback from our righteous false motivation.

Our people appeared. It was time to get back inside. But it was then that the most glorious thing happened.

A note on military wives: the officer wife and the enlisted wife are often substantially different subspecies. The officer wife is one to brag about how she had met her husband (now an O-3 and a motor transport officer) somewhere in 2D FSSG[31] when she was a college cheerleader and him a quarterback for Auburn. She somehow maintains an existence determined to be unaffected by the dragnet of the military town life. With a fresh pedicure and some Ashtanga yoga under her belt, she may be seen gliding throughout the PX[32] with a smile still reflecting the romantic wedding photos of her and her warrior-poet hubby in his dress uniform. Christmas cards with a cute little "Semper Fi" in golden cursive, a Lexus parked outside the commissary, and occasionally assuming her husband's rank among the other wives in her husband's unit, the officer wife is some strange sorority girl, all grown up, and can make a person forget they are in one of the finest institutions in the world for breeding anger, OCD, and risk intolerance.

The enlisted wife, however, is a whole other gallon of piss in the water bull. Having met her husband when he was an E-2, back from his first deployment, and buying a sports car at 50 percent APR, she has seen the side of the Corps left out of the recruiting posters. Gaining one child and fifteen pounds per husband's deployment, she can be seen in the Taurus with a hood not matching the paint job of the rest of the car,

---

31   Force Service Support Group
32   Post Exchange; convenient store on military bases

squeaking past you and yelling, "Slow down! Do you know who the fuck my husband is?!" as your eyes catch a sticker: a bouquet of flowers and the words "Marine Wife: toughest job in the Corps." Dumpy, pissed off, and with crimped hair, the enlisted wife is often both a source of never-ending hilarity as well as a penis depot when her federal paycheck provider is OCONUS[33].

The arrival of the enlisted wives, dressed to the nines in the hopes of getting plowed by some J-Ville farmer, all on their deployed husband's dollar, immediately caught our attention. Derrick, being the natural point man that he was, started the movement toward them.

"Excuse me, ladies," he said. "Would any of you like to dance with a United States Marine?"

A group of penguins standing on their small block of ice, dressed like hookers and laughing like hyenas: "What the fuck!?"

"Are you in MCT[34] or something?!" Derrick snapped to the position of attention, allowing them to shower him with insults fueled by loathing and boxed wine. "You are fucking pathetic— look at you," one burst.

I couldn't just leave him there, taking it from those glacial Dependapotami[35]. "Hey!" I yelled, then set them straight. "We are going to be grunts soon; we are in ITB[36]."

"Oh, my fucking god, you guys are fucking losers." It continued. "Big men. Biiggg Men."

33   Outside the contiguous United States; CONUS means within the contiguous United States
34   Marine Combat Training: portion of SOI designated for non-infantry students
35   Plural form for Dependapotamus: a parasitic military wife, generally to the enlisted, whose ratio of labor to benefits is asymmetrical; her normal stratagem is one child per spouse's deployment or enlistment, whichever is of the greater value
36   Infantry Training Battalion: portion of SOI designated for infantry students

The blatant irony, flying under the radar of the departing gaggle, was that we were making fun of the entire culture, by complete belligerent satire. Those who joined one of the most beloved fighting forces in all of human history just to run screaming to the first non-combat position available. Those who hid behind rank, or capitalized on the mythos of the Marines, while doing next to nothing to preserve it. Those who looked at the US military as a welfare check with a stupid haircut; the disgusting, bloated out-of-towners; the hilarious and harmless boots; and the whole damn shit show.

We reentered.

With our full party gathered and the beer really setting in, all I recall next was Derrick and me boogying with a bunch of girls on the dance floor. Many got such a kick out of our ensemble that we were approached like a blue light special.

And of course, I fell in love. Wedged between two women, being held together like a slowly swaying sandwich, about to come unglued at the first abrupt turn, I...nay, we slow danced as some twangy, cliché, country love ballad was playing. Our late group, nowhere as drunk or brazen, stood sober, likely in disgusted amazement, as I serenaded the two of them by singing along with the song: "And I'llllll beeee your maaaannnnnn."

The drunken Recon Boots split up. I left with my two dance partners and a bald guy one had picked up. Ending up in some trailer, of course, I face-planted into the hairiest muff of my career. The next day, the bald guy (who had ended up with the other gal) gave me a ride back to Courthouse Bay. It was not really an awkward ride in the traditional sense, but I learned he was a grunt, teaching at SOI, and that he failed the underwater swim during the Recon screening.

A few weeks later I received a call. An extremely hickish "Is this Day-vud?" was on the other end. I recognized the voice immediately: the unruly-bush owner. I hung up and wiped my phone with rubbing alcohol. Afterward, I continued prepping my gear for a few days out in the field.

7

HEARTS AND MINDS

*The United States and its Coalition partners are attempting to win the
hearts and minds of the people in Iraq...*

—Congressional Hearing, June 2004

Two in the heart, one in the mind.

—Smirking twenty-year-old tool of foreign policy, holding a
5.56×45-millimeter NATO cartridge, July 2004

FALL 2004

SCATTERED OUTSIDE THE FRONT entrance of the Iraqi
home, as the rest of my platoon waited on the road
for the wrecker, we had several military-aged males in
custody. Nighttime. The air had a faint, familiar chill to
it. It was a night like the ones in Georgia, when my mother would
have us stay with her relatives in the old manor. I could have been
under the giant magnolias, had it not been for the pistol being
forced into the detainee's mouth.

The IED had exploded, taking flesh, life, and limb. Right
before dark, from the other side of the Euphrates, a minaret had
emitted the evening prayer. Our brand-new platoon sergeant,
attached to the convoy that would be our original platoon sergeant's
final, was anything but "new." As a lone open-back Humvee sped
off with our injured (and our platoon commander), he stepped

down from some obscure senior enlisted administrative position, and in a moment returned to what he did best.

He also observed what I induced: the detonation point of the bomb perfectly aligned with a telephone pole when viewed from the minaret, which had eerily turned to a ruckus soon after the blast. We had driven like a row of paper dolls, and the detonator targeted our rear vehicle. Unable to reach the tower, we could, however, reach the house owning the front yard that had contained the IED. Not really a yard in the common understanding of the term, more the land that happened to occupy the physical space between the front of the house and the berm we had menacingly descended. On the sandy lawn, spread about like the sporadic shrubberies, an assortment of my platoons more frustrated or sadistic were down to assist in Gunny's[37] interrogation.

There was no method, only rage. We had spent months slogging through the province, raiding houses, and all we had to show for it were a couple of gunfights, mortar impacts all around us, and a few KIA[38] from bullshit indirect fire. I wanted my hands on someone, and I think most of my platoon was in thousand-yard agreement.

Five men pulled out of the house; it didn't take long. The one sitting closest to me: kicked in his lower back until my left foot ached in pain. The one with the pistol in his reluctant bearded mouth: on his back and mumbling Arabic words around the metal. A young one, late-teen perhaps, said aloud, "No, I won't talk," in proficient enough English to warrant Gunny's undivided attention. With our interpreter in tow, he had the recalcitrant bi-linguist off his feet, pinned against the wall. All around, one-sided skirmishes erupted. A muzzle thump here, choke hold there—even the interpreter got in a bitch slap. The

---

37   Marine short-hand for gunnery sergeant; E-7
38   Killed in action

air cooled as a breeze came in off the river, working its way through the body armor and tickling my spine.

Each marine wore his NVGs[39]. In these moments the world is shades of green and black. There is a paradoxical sense of both detachment and encapsulation that easily overwhelms anyone looking at the world this way—a claustrophobia that, once embraced, results in a comfortable loneliness. Special operations units overwhelmingly work at night. When night vision becomes standard vision, for some, solipsism embeds into the technical craft that fills the hours of our clandestine work. When a particular strike to a detainee resulted in a platoon mate exclaiming, "Damn, Rose," he could have been talking to a bush of the same nomenclature on the other side of the world.

I was wearing PVS-15s—aviator NVGS. They were excellent for driving, but while mobilizing on foot it took just a moment to refocus the depth. On this night, occupied by a frustration that stuck to the back of one's teeth, then consumed after by the thrill of physical retribution, I had forgotten to adjust them fully.

The detainees knew something: if they didn't detonate it, they buried it for the detonator; if they didn't bury it, they knew who did. After the rumble, Gunny wanted them segregated. All detainees were marched past me, single file, one at a time. It was because of some small ditch, or outer wall—I can't remember which, and it didn't matter. I just took advantage of the position. The first one was being escorted right by me. As I held my rifle with my right hand, I rocketed a left hook, coming from the hips and toward the first detainee's face. Unfortunately for the marine escorting him, the same guy who a moment prior had him sucking on his M9 Beretta, the unadjusted depth of my NVGs became

---

39   Night vision goggles

painfully known. I whiffed right past the detainee's head and landed my index knuckle square in the eye socket of his captor.

"O shit! I...I'm sorry, dude," I said.

"Fuck!"

"For real, bro, I am so fuckin' sorry." After a moment, "You can punch me in the face if it makes you feel better."

"No. Just—ugh!"

After an extremely awkward pause, he collected himself, resuming his walk past me, holding the bewildered, zip-tied Iraqi's arms with one hand, holding his face with the other. I adjusted my NVGs, already putting together my timid full apology for later.

As his curses and low murmurs faded into the distance, I saw the next one coming my way. Adjusting my footing, I bounced up and down to sort of get my confidence back. This next bearded face was going to receive it for the both of them.

There is little sensation that resembles the breaking of nose cartilage. Bludgeoned by the weapon of choice, if the weapon happens to be a part of your body, you can feel the give of hard tissue, followed by a crisp, nauseating crack.

<hr />

TRUTH BE TOLD, I haven't the foggiest idea what information, if any, our platoon extracted from those men. If those men weren't fighting against us already, they probably joined the opposing team soon after. Creating insurgency through collateral damage and bad PR was just the reality there.

At some point, they were released, sent limping back to their house as we ascended the berm and rejoined the rest of our platoon. I surveyed the damage of the IED blast. The targeted Humvee looked like a green, sand- and dust-covered dog that had been put to sleep. A few of its doors were open, one missing; the passenger side of the Humvee was bent in, making a deformed boomerang shape on the hardball. For some reason the wrecker and our horrendously late QRF[40] were arriving at the same time, the former from the west and the latter from the east. Back on the hardball, a couple of dim streetlights hung over our vehicles. NVGs off, some opened cans of chewing tobacco, some explained to the others who stayed with the vehicles what had transpired in the violent darkness. The QRF vehicles couldn't be seen, but in the stillness their diesel-engine rumbles could be heard. Only a few more twists and turns and they would emerge at the rear of our convoy.

Shots rang out.

The fuckhead enemy had been armed, lying in wait while we were distracted playing Gestapo.

Covering behind an open Humvee door, I looked for a muzzle flash. Nothing. Was it just more pop shots, some Iraqi with an AK-47 hoping to score a lucky hit? Buttstock in the pocket of my shoulder, barrel to the road, I hoped and prayed the same people responsible for maiming our platoon were about to make their presence known. A voice suddenly came over the radio. *Uh-huh, Uh-huh…Roger.* Our QRF had shot a vehicle that had been quickly approaching them. Operating within the ROE[41], they protected their lives from the very legitimate threat of VBIEDs[42]. It was a family in the shot-up vehicle. A five-year-old had been shot and killed.

---

40   Quick reaction force
41   Rules of engagement: aside from getting servicemen killed, it theoretical-ly functions as a framework for order and a moral code in the combat setting
42   Vehicle-borne improvised explosive device

The wrecker arrived, and along with it the cold. Sapped of aggression and replaced with the dull weariness that often overtakes a combat zone, time dragged achingly. Other than a few dark shapes walking up and down the road, and the wrecker crew hooking up our destroyed Humvee, people ossified in the seats and turrets. The cold was so intense that night. It had a way of undressing you. Finally, the wrecker was ready to go, and the convoy of Triton 2, QRF, the laden wrecker, and the wrecker's security began to make the long trek back to Camp Fallujah. Canals I had seen many times in daylight looked different that night. The shades of green seemed to capture the cold, making everything look ancient and alien. Crawling past landmarks and tiny villages, the occasional voice cracked through the radio. We saw the front gate around dawn.

Word had long since reached our battalion about the hit we took. The injured had arrived there many hours prior, some of whom had already landed in Baghdad for surgery. Humvees parked in our motor pool, gear brought into our team room; our first sergeant met us at the door with tin-foil-wrapped dinners. The night before had been Thanksgiving, a thing that meant something to some people. I had forgotten all about it, and it wasn't until the following Thanksgiving, this time at my aunt's house, that it meant anything at all. Not the stupidity of celebrating pagans teaching zealots how to grow corn, nor the food or the football, but that the day itself was connected forever to an extraordinary memory.

Taking my plate from my first sergeant's hand, I heard Derrick say from behind, "Fuck that—I don't want his pity." I didn't either, I thought, as I bit into the white meat.

OUR ORIGINAL PLATOON SERGEANT got it the worst, making it all the way to Germany before finally succumbing to his wounds. Not long after was the funeral, held in camp and put together with cheap recording equipment, particle board, and one large, haunting printout of our dead. The night before, three other guys and I snorted a bunch of Adderall. A platoon mate had his sister mail it occasionally. He said it helped him stay awake on the turret for the lengthy night-movements. We had chopped, snorted, and talked amid my extremely focused and one-time-only poetry readings until it was dawn. Suddenly in a formation, the ceremony was a suspended, electrified freak-out. Staring at the mural of the fallen, synthetic meth still pumped through me—a wide-eyed statue of jaw-clenched insomnia.

Twelve hours later, without so much as a cat nap, we were tasked to go on a twenty-four-hour mission. Driving outside the wire, PVS-15s donned, I wasn't certain I was ever going to sleep again. As best I could, I calibrated my general duties: breaks, accelerator, gear shifter, safety, fire, full automatic, pull pin, and throw the heavy part... Just about the moment I was ready to pray to God for some halting intervention, Allah beat him to the punch. Our attachments, some army cavalry guys, flipped their Humvee and several had broken ribs. We returned home. The mission was aborted. I fell asleep two days later.

8

FUCK YOU, POGS?

SUMMER 2003

POG: noun \'pōg\: acronym for personnel other than grunt.

Note (confessions of a former POG): a sadistic and shady recruiter, who could not pronounce the word 'ask,' changed my infantry contract to "open contract" so as to allow me to go to boot camp early. I found this out at MEPS[43], and spent all of boot camp fighting the forces of evil from obliging me to be a "data systems specialist," whatever that means. Nine days prior to graduation, I was pulled into a master sergeant's office to go over my ASVAB score and potential career paths. Practically in tears, and staring with almost religious fascination at the chevrons on his sleeves, I was able to muster the words, "This recruit only joined the Marines to go infantry, sir." At this, the old lifer stopped typing, leaned back in his chair, and looked up at the ceiling, almost as if out on a walk and stopping to take in the smell of fresh cut grass. He turned to me and said, "Son, I started in the air wing, and looking back I wish I had started out in the infantry." I could see the regret in his eyes. A few mouse clicks later, I ended up in artillery. Non-infantry yes, but a lot damn closer to the fight than a fucking data systems specialist.

---

43   Military Entrance Processing Command

Being in artillery was existing in middle ground. In one sense I was in a regiment, meaning change of command ceremonies, Chinese field days, and tired speeches from first sergeants six months from retirement. It also meant I was just a number, and a goddamn low one at that. An E-2 in a full regiment is a worker bee: nameless, expendable, and good for one thing. The artillery regiment shares the lifestyle of the infantry regiment, as far as garrison duties and annoyances go. But, while no doubt brutal and tried and true in combat, artillery is not infantry.

Taken in literal form, POG is blunt and broad. It is important to understand that when used derogatorily, as it always is, it is never meant to encompass fighter pilots, forward observers, or medics and corpsmen in the shit, stepping it out with the ruck-humpers. Nor is it really to shame those who felt of better use elsewhere.

There have always been and always will be folks who fall under POG yet garner their rightful respect. Arguably, this is achieved through the combination of their job efficiency and willingness to join in the muck and the misery. The support is both realized and appreciated—but hey, shake a military hand and expect a buzzer. When POG is unsheathed, it is almost always done as an ancient reminder to some without the stomach to uphold the fierce warrior ethos, yet demands to benefit from its image at the job interview, the bar, Tinder, and the high school reunion.

And oh how much it was, and is, demanded. This doesn't just apply to the veteran community, of course, but actually stems from a sort of institutional communism the Marine Corps specifically possesses.

Marx must be in his cenotaph laughing his fuckin' dick off. The saviors of the American Way, these brave young men kissing their high school sweethearts goodbye to defend the nuclear family, Jesus, and the McRib from those godless Commies—all to employ some classic Communist propaganda into their esprit de corps.

And for a moment it is prudent to explain further:

Every marine is, first and foremost, a rifleman. All other conditions are secondary.

—General Alfred M. Gray, USMC

The shortened version is "Every Marine a Rifleman." It's from this bumper sticker slogan that the *original sin* of the USMC germinates.

What is true is the Marines systemically function as infantry-centric. An example is seen in Marine aviation, which has retained its focus on CAS[44] despite opposing military theories that propose strategic bombing as tactically superior to close air support. It's also true that every enlisted marine goes through some infantry training and every marine officer goes through training as an infantry platoon commander.

However, the romance ends there. Speaking only from the enlisted perspective, all marines who are non-infantry (*gasp,* that's correct kids...in fact, most marines are non-infantry... like dutiful mechanics and administrative desk monkeys) go through a three-week crash course, known deceptively as Marine Combat Training.

MCT: This disaster, at least for me, was a place where following MRE trash got you a passing score on a land navigation course, where getting to pound out a single belt of ammo gets you "familiar" with a crew-served weapon. The ruck marches can kick an ass or three, and as your grenade sump fills with water in the fighting hole you and another POG took all day to dig, you get to see exactly how shitty the grunt life would have been.

The grunt world is just categorically different than the others that orbit it. This is best illustrated in a spectrum.

---

44   Close air support

Garrison:

As stated above, the regimental lifestyle maintains certain unnegotiable tenets. Whether a grunt or a POG, a Thursday field day (something that would blow the mind of an uninitiated civilian, peering into the depths of anal retentiveness and OCD that seem to serve as the glue used by senior enlisted) is basically the same thing. We all have to obey base speed limits, base uniform regulations, and the like. Here, the distinctions are at their slightest, and of course here is where most service members make it their career. It is no wonder illogical perceptions like "Every marine a..." come forth from the garrison setting. In garrison, a person's shooting ability and ability to work under duress—including lack of sleep and environmental extremes—don't get exposed. But how nice a uniform is, or who has the most immaculate, shining high and tight haircut, these are things that the garrison setting allows to be seen.

And then of course there is the reaction from the civilian world. It was enough to induce violent vomiting spasms when some sorority girl, with a confused stare like an overbred dog and a bleached asshole, would say something to the beat of, "He looks like a marine, but you kinda don't." Fragile male egos decimated worse than if hit by an RPG. She was referring of course to the guy who worked a chair at base admin and was two hundred and ten pounds of unhindered, paper-shuffling garrison muscle, whilst you...lowly, and wretched you...had just ended thirty consecutive days in the field. Your arms skinny from inaction, and the MREs giving you that godforsaken spare tire.

The rifleman, whether apt for central casting or not, is the rifleman. Because the clean cammies and untested physiques would be covered in algae or desert dust if in the field, and possibly covered in blood and shit if out in a combat theater.

Field:

The "field," to those unversed, simply refers to being outside, and to be training in some capacity. The first fact that should jump out to a sensible observer is that a lot of people in the military don't go to this field at all. Bingo.

This means available gym time is drastically different for service members who go to the field regularly, those who do occasionally, and those who never go at all. The juxtaposition of all the military details of humanity—the burly, ripped marines on the posters and fighting mythical creatures on TV—are in fact typing at a desk or counting MRE boxes in a Quadcon[45] when the media is released.

However, many non-infantry military do go to the field. Here the distinctions start to stretch. For one, the support roles for the infantry generally are static. A field chow hall, supply tent, water site, etc., are all static as a means of being operational. Granted these sites can and do move, done with vehicles; however, once the new point is reached, static operations recommence. This is significant because the POG-in-field is generally sheltered from the elements. The monsoon/scorching-sun cycle is a particular favorite of those who train in places like Okinawa or the southeastern United States.

Aggregate months of chiggers, swamp ass, and the ruck marches that draw blood—these create a very different psychological being.

There is nothing like a pissed-off lance corporal: nineteen, clean rifle, a little tired, and angry at the world.

—A Marine Corps sergeant major before speeding off in his F350

---

45   Large ground container used by the US military

Combat Theater:

And finally we arrive at the great divider: a bona fide armed conflict. Both garrison and field settings are where military training is conducted. The most simple but powerful distinction is thus: the infantry is meant to kill an enemy, and usually does so on foot. An astute critic would correctly point out that artillery, tanks, F-18s, etc., are also meant solely to kill the enemy. While true, the profound difference is the mode in which this is carried out. When I was in artillery, the motto "If you can't truck it, fuck it" was adhered to like gender segregation at the Wailing Wall circa 1955. Trucks have wheels, planes have wings, the infantry has feet. Whether dropped out of an aircraft or given a ride in an Amtrak, the good work of the grunt is eventually done in a pair of worn boots.

Iraq is an example. Much like jobs that take one out into the field, only certain military occupations require one to leave the wire. Personally, I always felt bad for those who never left. I would have gone stir crazy and couldn't help but imagine they all felt they were missing out on all the fun. That hypothesis was dismissed the moment we started getting large attachments around the time of Operation Phantom Fury. One case that sticks out was an engineer who refused to get out of the back of a five-ton truck. Chanting over and over, "If I get out of this truck I'm going to die, if I get out of this truck I'm going to die," the pubescent was soon ripped off the bench by an unsympathetic platoon sergeant. To my knowledge he lived, but his intuition was rather ominous. Only several days after this little display of prophetic cowardice, engineers attached to us would start getting killed and injured at a bizarre rate. While our teams were staying whole, for the most part, our attachments were getting beat to shit. It was rumored that at the conflict's height, they were refusing to go out with us, which may have been true to some extent considering we ended up getting their sergeants as long-term attachments, who were likely (possibly reluctantly) "leading from the front."

Of all who operate in the battle space—infantry, motor transport, engineers, pilots—the infantry is the undisputed king of time outside the wire. Anywhere from days to months, a grunt lives in jungles, snow, deserts, and seized houses.

Lastly, infantry has the closest proximity to the enemy when combat occurs. Front lines, tip of the spear, forward area—you name it—unless someone fucks up somewhere, which happens, it is the infantry that goes blow to blow with combatants. This is a general rule, therefore not absolute. History is littered with contrary cases. Combat engineers, medical personnel, and, in extreme circumstances, cooks and clerks have all lived or died with bayonet, ammo can, or entrenching tool in their hands as the last weapon available. What is important here is a return to military theory. The significance of proximity to the enemy is that the infantry is intended to be. This detail cannot be overstated; the grunt goes into the fray, knowing full good and well it will be he and the men of his ilk who will come face to face with…it.

MORNING, HEADQUARTERS BATTERY FOR the 10th Marine Artillery Regiment is running down Julian C. Smith Boulevard in Camp Lejeune, North Carolina. Surveyors, Artillery Meteorological, Counter Battery Radar, Comm, Motor T, and Marine Corps admin all running and calling out cadence. This running formation was led by a genetically gifted woman. By all accounts she was a fine marine—professional demeanor—later left to be a drill instructor. This proud group approaches a T intersection. In this very formation jogs a future—well, what some may call a gunslinger. Stuck in the middle of this slow-moving monster, out of the corner of my eye I notice a soggy, angry, giant millipede, green and metal, crawling steadily up to the intersection as well.

It is grunts!

Dirty, stupid, bullet-sponge grunts! They are conducting a ruck march, wet from sweat and a predawn rain that our group had missed by several hours. Perpendicular to the road we are on, our formations are coming to an inevitable collision.

The military has all sorts of customs and courtesies, some of which are abided by more religiously than others. The Marine Corps is notorious for right-of-way-related rules, as well as anything remotely dealing with safety. For instance, while entering and exiting vehicles, the junior ranking member is the first to enter, and the senior is the first to exit.

My mind begins to spin—what is going to happen?—and I begin to smile as the question is answered.

Bursting through, the commanding officer of the grunt unit severs us in half with his men.

The grunts—a little skinny, a little tired, tattoos exposed through weather-beaten camouflage, mortar plates, rucks, and crew-served weapons—flick us off as they march forth, screaming, "Fuck you, POGs!"

The endowed sergeant leading our run, reduced to hugging the side of our stalled formation like a tree frog, winces and flinches at the catcalls as if they are globules of spit.

How I envied them, this passing horde of war-machine profanity. How I knew I had to leave artillery and join their ranks, or otherwise I would have been severely cheated out of a damn good time.

9

MYRTLE BEACH

There is such a thing as a 'natural soldier': the kind who derives his greatest satisfaction from male companionship, from excitement, and from the conquering of physical obstacles.

—Gwynne Dyer, *War*

SPRING 2004

ORT POLK, LOUISIANA, HOME of the Joint Readiness Training Center; a vast particle-board city dedicated to urban operations—and within it, 2D Recon Bn had spent the past few weeks engaged in furious (battery-tampered) MILES[46] shoot-outs, or conducting OPs in the drenched, snake-infested woods on its outskirts. After the escalating training exercises, frequent lightning strikes, and a booze-fueled closing party with the Army Ranger cadre, our battalion went back to North Carolina.

There is something about several weeks of repetition that invigorates the need to go out and let loose, to break off a piece of lay or just be piss drunk in some over-cushioned bed. A group coalesced: a plan formulated, bags packed, bodies stuffed into a jeep, five guys and I tore out of Camp Lejeune. Myrtle Beach was our destination. With another car packed full shortly behind us, we were going to a condo owned by the parents of one of our own

---

Multiple Integrated Laser Engagement System

in attendance. A special perk of this weekend getaway was that it was the first time a handful of us got to party with two of our former RIP instructors. We had completed RIP, graduated ARS, and had spent a little bit of time in the battalion, and now we got to throw down with these righteous dudes. It was so cool; the dynamic of instructor/student dissolved instantly and in its place was the dynamic of senior operator/junior operator. However, that didn't mean some sort of stereotypical stiff hierarchy was in place. An exalted brotherhood permeated in the jeep, drinking beer and laughing hysterically about anything from an embarrassing high school story to how the two had hazed the rest of us while we were paying our dues.

The journey there was a blur of passing beer cans, getting wild with the grab-ass, and weaving fast through traffic, concerned only with getting laid and avoiding being the *libo incident.*

Flash to a packed nightclub:

Cholo, one of the RIP instructors, was one of the only Hispanic recon marines in our unit at the time. He had been the one I recited the final paragraph of the Creed to when I'd first arrived. Since then, I'd learned his name and his ways. He loved being a gatekeeper, and possessing a slight sadistic streak, his round face emitted a certain smile whenever a subordinate required *correction.* But this was no night for such...machismo. Cholo pulled out his freshest moves on the dance floor with carefully timed spins in front of his targets.

Adam, the other RIP instructor, was equally a work of art. Tattooed and built like the leader of a group of soccer hooligans, shot out of a cannon from some Massachusetts town, his energy and appearance could be menacing. That was until you spent a minute around him. For all the potential brutishness, he was one of the funniest and most easygoing operators one could ever meet. He was able to do the rare balancing act of emitting almost constant humor while taking the work seriously. Having those around you acknowledge this efficiency was rare, but he somehow did it. Adam was also kicking it on the dance floor; however, he'd gone with the economy of motion theorem and picked up a blonde cougar, rawboned, in a miniskirt, and vaguely reminiscent of that televangelist wife with the forty-pound hair.

And then there was Chris. He was the one who'd recited the second paragraph of the Creed that morning. Like Adam, Chris hailed from Massachusetts. Without question, that state, for whatever reason, produced some of the hardest hitters. Chris was invulnerable when it came to the physical aspects of the job. During a team log run, he'd have almost the entire weight of the trunk on his shoulder, being taller than most the others—who were trying to pitch in and carry their share by pressing upward on the log with both hands. Fin work; I had the pleasure of being pulled by him, kilometer after kilometer. Wrestling, running, ruck marches, all just brief occupiers of time; requiring a slight deviation from his ultimate frat-boy existence. CKY, Metallica, and orgasmic screams from young women erupted in frequent burst from his barracks room.

Chris had already gotten kicked out of the club twice and snuck back in the same. Our other guys were on the periphery, talking to girls, taking shots, and sporting the cleanest clothes they'd worn in over a month. I wandered around the edge of the dance floor, got blasted in the face by a hidden mist machine, and made my way to the bathroom to yet again unload the results of my love for the hops.

Relieving myself at a urinal, I got shoved into it. "Hey, faggot," Chris said while carefully placing his beer bottle on the chrome piping of his own urinal. I would have expressed disdain that the head of my dick had just stamped the fetid urinal wall if it weren't for the distracting mob of bouncers that came rushing in.

"How many times do we gotta fuckin tell ya shitheaddddd?!"

"Yeah, that fuckers back again."

"Get him!"

Chris was put in a whirlwind of shaved arms, black shirts, and curses as his unsecured dick flapped about. Falling back on his training, he grabbed his beer and zipped up his pants simultaneously. The coordination was that of a professional juggler, I thought, as I watched them drag him off the tile and out into the main lobby.

Stowing my own member and biting my bottom lip, I proceeded out after him. In a matter of seconds some of our brothers had appeared and were trying to reason with the swarm. Chris, holding his beer like the Statue of Liberty, was keeping at bay the circle of increasingly determined bouncers. He looked like a leopard, mouth open and hissing at a group of baboons on the offensive.

No time for diplomacy, I grabbed the closest one, an approaching reinforcement ascending the stairs from the dance floor. His attempt at tackling me opportunely put my left forearm under his chin, which made for a glorious, feet-lifting choke hold as he dangled on the last several steps of the staircase. This Napoleonic security official swung to and fro as his goatee rubbed against my favorite tattoo, and his fists on my legs and body fell so short of hurting.

Before "it" happened, I remember one of our own pleading for me to let him go, and that I was only making matters worse. Suddenly, some horizontal object, the shade of white, hung suspended in my sight. I thought, *How odd a thing to see.*

Next thing I knew, I was on the carpet, pinned, cheek smashed to the floor with someone's boot on my head. "You give up? Yeah—you fuckin' give the fuck up," someone said, with a very precise face-shove into the floor. I had been clotheslined by a monster among their staff. As I lay there, the one whom I'd made struggle so valiantly on the stairs had to be held back by several others. From my angle, he may have been crying, tears of frustration maybe, or it may have been a sporadic douse from Chris's wildly protected beer bottle.

Like an old black and white movie, or western with a comedic flare, Chris and I were literally thrown out. Two bags of human-limbed trash were heaved out the front door and dumped to the ground at the feet of a group of hot college freshmen types. In my short flight, I had almost careened headfirst into a hot dog vendor. I was in no mood for such embarrassment in front of zombie-eyed blondes, stolid in heels, standing almost in a formation with one predesignated, hideous fat friend in the pack. Slowly rising up off my back and rolling up and onto a shoulder, I was eye level with all those supple, shaved legs. I licked my lips, unnerving both one bouncer and one girl—pussy.

In no mood, Chris and I, in some instant wordless agreement, sprang up and crashed into the wall of bouncers dutifully guarding the vulnerable entrance. A few punches were thrown, and a "you're so tough with your ponytail and your one earring, you fat faggot" was spewed at a middle-aged one. A hand grabbed my Adam's apple, and just prior to admitting defeat Chris bounced into the picket line, sprawled out like an *X*.

We were done. Cholo came out of the club and started pushing our chests—Chris, me, Chris, me—a demented game of checkers, back to the jeep.

"Jesus fucking Christ, guys," said Cholo, walking back inside. I watched him fix his collar and softly sculpt his hair with the palms of his hands, and the irrefutable feeling came over me: that was fucking amazing! As we leaned on the jeep to laugh until our ribs hurt, it didn't take long to find Adam passed out in the backseat with his cougar. Neither would stir no matter how hard we banged or yelled.

Locked out of the jeep and banished from the club, blood pumping too hard to do anything remotely rational, we decided to walk back to the front entrance. We had a corner to round and then had to make our way past some concealment—then we would most certainly cause a hilarious and violent reaction. Prior to rounding the first corner, I noticed a side door wide open. Chris had some gaze in his eyes and was looking straight forward like a marathon runner. I let him go ahead. Slipping inside the doorway, I set my eyes on a small, red box on the wall, one whose potential interaction with my fingers titillated a surging anarchistic fantasy.

The patrons filed out in their upset march, Mariveles to San Fernando, draped in department store cuteness and sweating from summer heat and the full effects of ecstasy.

All accounted for, our convoy got back to the condo. The next day I gleefully broke the news of causing the code-enforced exodus. Laughs and an "it's cool, we were ready to go anyway, hell I didn't have to pay for that last round because of it, fuck yeah" was about the extent of it. That was last night and we now had more pressing matters at hand. Apparently someone had made contact with a group of girls from UNC at the club and we were all getting together for a lunch.

It was about what I expected: a crowded bench table overflowing with specials and buckets of beer, Chris and Lane landing future lays while I dozed off as one of the girls talked to me about something I couldn't recall a moment after.

After lunch we splintered into smaller groups, hoping to knock out our own wish lists, then meet up at the condo later. Four of us left the restaurant in the car that had followed the jeep up the day prior.

We were at a red light, stuck at a congested midday intersection. Sitting in the backseat, my ears began to pick up a screeching, pummeling noise—ending before it had even fully registered.

An SUV careened the rear of the car next to us, exploding the back half. This lethal weapon, come to an abrupt and violent halt, was being driven by the type of drunk woman one would expect to see commit a hit-and-run at a Walmart.

"Yeah!" burst from my mouth as I punched the headrest in front of me a few times. All of us quickly got out of the car and surveyed the tangled metal chaos. It spit gasoline, had a stuck horn, and a left rear blinker that looked about ready to throw out a spark. The occupants were an old couple. They stirred about in their seats, staring out the windows without blinking. The old-timer pushed against his door like a feeble child, or a recon marine after drinking a case of beer the night before stalks at sniper school in Stone Bay in July. Pulling and pulling on the outside handle, its stubbornness must have been a result of the crash. The car was completely locked, with gas leaking and some accessories still churning. The old man then gave me a look, almost a nod, giving me some sort of impetus to act.

A few years prior, at a Halloween party back home gone terribly awry, I discovered my knack for breaking car windows with a horizontal, hip-engined elbow strike. I got my footing. His look of bewilderment only intensified as the glass burst around his face.

"Just get my wife out," he pled, as I leaned over him into the car, unbuckling his seatbelt, and ripped him out through the shattered window. The smell of gas and sparky noises was not lost on me. Leaning back inside the car, this time much farther, I couldn't undo her seatbelt, nor convey the verbiage necessary for her to do it herself. I scurried out and ran around to her door. Approaching EMS sirens made their way through the rubbernecking.

Her window had to have been made of something different. With my forearm cut from breaking her husband's window, blood slung about as I beat against the glass in vain. It was a skinny black kid, equipped in the urban regalia of a wife-beater tank top and cornrows, who dove in and fished her out of the driver's side window. He was gone before the first cop car arrived. Was he an angel? Late for an appointment perhaps? Did he know from experience that his altruistic act wouldn't matter worth a shit if a cop ran his ID and discovered the warrant?

"THIS GUY, THIS GUY's the man, bustin' through a window like that with a fist," said one paramedic to another. The portly Hispanic man wrapped my left hand as the old folks were taken into an ambulance on stretchers. He looked up at me. "You're gonna have to go to the hospital too, sir. We can't do anything for that cut." *That cut* was a two-angle avulsion, almost a perfect right angle, which somehow grabbed a piece of the breaking window as it was in the process of shattering. After a Comm plan was made with the rest of the guys, and a shoulder shrug later, I was in an ambulance of my own.

Placed in a general ER waiting room, I saw another old couple. My hand started to sting and blood was showing through the white. The old man, through a thick set of glasses, was scanning my arms. Nothing uncommon. It was usually the very young and the very old who looked at my ink, and then the man wearing it, in the way I'd originally envisioned at sixteen when I got my first one. His expression suddenly changed to that of a person figuring out that troublesome row of a crossword puzzle. Our eyes met. He smiled—endearingly, proprietary. An instant connection melted away so many things right then, his extreme age included. How I've seen this, as have others; a meeting of American warriors melts away the paltry details forcefully given to us by time.

Truth be told, this phenomena is not limited to something finite as "American." I am sure generations of military in other countries have similar if not exact sentiments as we have. Hell, and of course we can't forget guerrilla fighters and terrorists. Some bearded Sunni, wounded in Ramadi in 2006, is undoubtedly adored by certain eighteen-year-old Iraqi males with the same palpable vigor and zeal that a private out of Marine Corps boot camp may have for an approaching commandant.

He spoke with a calm southern accent à la Andy Griffith. "How long you been in the Corps, son?"

"About two years. Were you in?" I knew the answer.

"That's what you were in," his wife said to him.

"I was a rifleman for the Second Marine Division," he said with a nod, crossing his arms.

He'd fought in WWII. And once the conversation was opened, the floodgate of gold-painted memories poured. Country visited here. Buddy lost there. Got sick the day he picked up Corporal and had to be flown one hundred and fifty miles to remove his appendix. Eventually I drifted. I was on some decimated Western Pacific island, old rifle in my hands.

"And then, son, I ended my time garrison on a flag-folding detail," he said.

"Oh, that is right," his wife said.

"It was an honor. The boys that died for that flag," he said.

It was more than acceptable for him to have done such a detail, the flag-folding—hell, it was almost cute. But somehow it rang true to me still, it was altogether proper for my generation of riflemen to scorn anyone doing such a job, and for no other reason than taking pride in something not on the front lines, or ahead of it.

Listening to his virtuous stance on "duty," my mind began to sink into my own moral conundrums.

It's a simple case of conflicting moral theory. The truth is I dashed out of our car and broke the window for the sheer excitement of doing so. Taking it all into consideration, was I a *good person* at all? Had I ever been? And how the more problematic when expanding the question to why I picked up the rifle for my nation.

A crash course in some of the main features within moral philosophy:

Deontology asserts that a moral agent is obliged by duty to others. This duty is a universal condition; therefore this theory aligns with the belief that *right* and *wrong* are objective. Deontologists will also generally argue that a moral agent's intentions are what determine if an action is right or wrong.

Utilitarianism asserts that a moral agent is obliged to act in a manner that does the greatest good and least harm. Proponents of utilitarianism generally argue that a moral agent's intentions do not determine whether an action was a "good act" or a bad act" but rather the end state.

Kant would have been so displeased with me, at least until I saw the fear in the man's eyes. Before that moment, I was acting only to pleasure my own senses and lifelong love affair with the sound of breaking glass. I was amused by the accident—energized by it, in fact.

But, even if self-serving, it got me out of the car and into the one that looked to be ready to go up in a gown of flames. While a strict deontologist would say my intent was worthy of no moral praise, my actions did achieve the greater good. However, the utilitarian would have nothing for my delayed but eventual desire to help them, only the fact that they were helped. Interestingly enough, if somehow my elbow strike resulted in a shard of glass cutting the carotid artery of the driver, killing him (and of course no fire occurred), then deontology would defend my actions via my good intentions, while utilitarianism would denounce the act as immoral.

Years later I found out that if I'd reported the event to my unit, I would've been put in for some high-caliber award that is only given for "heroic" actions by marines outside of combat zones. I never reported it, nor said a word to anyone, save the guys who watched the ambulances speed away.

WITH ALL OF US back at the condo, and on the eve of our return to Camp Lejeune, Adam decided to perform one of the most famous histrionics in all of Recon.

Dick tricks: the act of manipulating the penis and scrotum to resemble persons, places, or things.

The Sail Boat. The Fat Kid on a Trampoline. A few more and then it was time for the iconic Cobra. I had heard rumor of it before. Most of us had. He had a tattoo of the damn thing on his arm.

Adam pissed up into his own mouth. The UNC girls stood motionless with their slight, nervous smiles. Personally, I think they were more taken aback by how entertaining all the rest of us thought it was. Usually the pop-collared, upwardly mobile college boys would do stuff like fallback on a pickup forum and express hyper-disdain for such provincial and gruff actions. But this was not the case. The same guys who'd wooed them at the club had since abandoned the status quo of identity crucifixion, the sexual political correctness, abandoned the subtleties, and were applauding Adam as if not one vagina was in sight.

Adam spewed the piss from his mouth, an explosive stream right at us...like a cobra.

10

HOSPITALS, WARDS, AND JAIL CELLS

Men have called me mad; but the question is not yet settled, whether madness is or is not the loftiest intelligence—whether much that is glorious—whether all that is profound—does not spring from disease of thought—from moods of mind exalted at the expense of the general intellect.

—Edgar Allen Poe, *Eleonora*

SUMMER 2011

MY SOJOURN IN A VA psych ward occurred during a period in my life that was as formidable in its pallid malaise as the hospital itself. Told that the ward was located under the Alzheimer's wing, I envisioned lunatics clawing and moaning at the ceiling while demented types clawed and moaned at the floor, talking in some terrible found language, wrought from their agreeable abnormalities.

Upon reaching the mopped floors of its entrance, I was no longer in control of my own destiny, and in fact hadn't been for some time. The claustrophobia of "custody" shook me a little as I passed under its shadowy arch.

That period in time, twisted and queer, became all the more so due to my need for numbness. I had always possessed a keen ability to turn so drastically inward in times of duress that I felt little, pain included. Occasionally referred to as "hard" or the possessor of great mental strength; for good or ill, this ability was what carried me so far. This time, however, I had completely sunk in my inversion. I wandered into oblivion and was perhaps rewarded at times for the dark trek. I needed to be numb. The realization, powder-burned into my face; my own shortcomings assisted in a swift crumble. I went from warrior to emotional unavailability, vicious irritability, and bouts of an unparalleled restlessness that would bend the very space and time around me. These unpleasant attributes had laid my former self in its tomb, and I had become the most senseless of wanderers.

When suicide inevitably places itself on the workbench, it is up to the individual. Some take it, some don't. For me and some others, a term, that to my knowledge I'm the original source for, has served as a motivator to stay in the land of the living. *Antaganomorphism*: assigning adversarial agency or behavior to phenomena with emphasis on obstacles and conflict. This gets so many through the bullshit. That Hemingway's pride of beating the odds, fighting the "it," sticking it to the impersonal "thems" of the world. The sensation of personally battling, outwitting, or convincing an opposing agent is a powerful internal mechanism to prove oneself, not to themselves but to an outside entity.

But what happens when that motivator dies, when that pride pushing your corpse through the ringer finally fades?

———◦———

BEYOND THE INCESSANT BUZZING of my GPS monitor and the lack of sleep, the only real annoyance with the ward was that the place had no sharp edges. It was some fun house of horrors designed to prevent suicide via hanging from the horizontal top of a door or apparently running into the corner of a wall. It wasn't long before I got in some nurse's face. My proclamation of discontent was soon followed by the administering of a mysterious and monstrous green pill. Thorazine maybe. Swallowing this pill and the subsequent swaying gait back to my room was the last moment of coherence for the next twelve hours or so.

In my room, alone and temporarily unmolested by the hourly well-being checks, I discovered there was a door in a far corner behind a small, rounded desk. Somehow it had eluded me the first few times I'd stormed in to sit on a rounded chair and clench my fists. Coming here had done nothing but make me realize how bad I wanted to leave. Perhaps the only feeling stronger just then was my curiosity.

Flinging open this door, I was standing at the entrance to an odd, long corridor, lighted by dull candelabras. Desire to leave the ward was replaced by a stiffening paranoia. Stepping inside and fighting an instant urge to turn and run, wanting to go only so far as to discern the end; yet it was impossible. The farthest lights showed nothing of the passage; they could have been stars suspended in a void, and I became certain they were exactly that. The passage led beyond the psych ward, beyond the hospital, beyond the city surrounding it, beyond the entirety of the Earth itself—to the land of Beyond—and of the dead.

A face appeared in the wall. My only reaction was to punch it. My hand sank into a viscous substance that felt nothing like drywall and particle board. Under a smothering mess of noise that sounded like engines whining, I heard a cry from the struck wall.

Looking back the way I had come, less than the number of steps to get from the nurses desk to the game room, my mind howled. A terrible distance stretched to the door I had entered from. Uniformly, and with cadence, the lights in the intervening spaces went out in turn. Trying to run back, the floor nauseously gave way to the pounding of my mired feet. I toiled as if in a fen. The walls emitted pitiful sighs, as their corners that joined the ceiling melted to become a tunnel, or maybe a tube.

Pops and gurgles, followed by smacking sounds, yanked my sight behind me. Protrusions in the wall writhed and undulated, occasionally separating from the original corpus, and flopped to the floor. Vague in shape, they crawled gawkily after me.

I fought these images with the desperate belief that it was all a superbly bizarre reaction to conflicting medication. Surprisingly it helped, but the black figure that stalked behind the wall's fetid spawn destroyed any remaining defensive tools of rationale. I averted my eyes, sure that if I gazed just a moment longer I would recognize it.

I uprooted my legs from the slimy base and dragged myself out of the tunnel's end. Fumbling from the prone to standing, I slammed the door, dry heaving at the thumps and soft hisses against the other side.

I awoke on my back. On the narrow hard bed assigned to me, my blouse was torn wide with my wet chest exposed; breathing the way a man does when rustled from a nightmare. I took in my surroundings, collected all the pieces, and then laid them out, scrutinizing the credulity of my senses. Looking over to my right, I saw that in my unconsciousness they had bequeathed to me a roommate.

Word had bounced back and forward, from nurse to patient alike, that a suicidal criminal with an ankle bracelet was to be housed on-site. Considering the place, which housed generations of combat veterans with a stunning brigade of mental health issues, one would think my presence would mean little. However, both the young doctor who referred to me as a "spent shell casing," and the Midwestern-pederast-looking social worker with all the pitiful acronyms, informed me of my celebrity status within the facility.

There for being a retard, or a fucking pussy, I can't remember which, this Baker Act was on the other bed in the room. Lying on his stomach and fighting an internal war—"keep looking at him because he already caught me staring, or look away now as a sign of courtesy, which improves my odds of not getting my neck bit"—etched itself into his face as his mouth hung wide. Blond, soft, and owning a ripe zit indicative of his young age, he froze in his nervousness.

"Are you going back to jail when you leave here?" he asked, looking at my ankle.

Looking at the sweat still beading on my skin, I replied, "You mean prison." It was hard not to smile. The pharmacological warp had run its course, returning me to the world where dark forces weren't found lurking in gooey tunnels, but rather in state-sanctioned paper trails. Fucking with this timid kid was the first enjoyable experience I had had thus far. He nodded absentmindedly, closed his mouth, turned his head away from me, and laid it down on his pillow.

The next day I would be let out, soon after experiencing the screeching halt that comes with instantaneously breaking away from high-dosage, mandatory antidepressants.

My last night in the ward was much different than the other. No green pill. No lurid, metaphysical wayfaring. I watched a group of veterans in psych ward scrubs play Monopoly into the wee hours of windowless morning. I heard a country song from the game room's high-bolted, box television that made me miss, all at once, a childhood I'd known and a woman who I'd never. But before all of that, before Whitechapel Road got a hotel,

Community Chest, or a Southern belle with traffic-light eyes sang about death, a barrel-chested army vet, who'd gloated how he'd been surrounded in a movie theatre by a SWAT team just two nights prior, took control of the snack cart line. He didn't fuck with the ankle bracelet man. I received the first PB&J, ensured my Beta-male roomie got his, and used the scenario to practice custodial politics for the real thing—in the big house—a fate that would not come to pass.

11

THE SNOW-BIRD

WINTER 2006

A H, THE SUMMERS AND springs outside the back gate of Camp Lejeune. In the warmer half of the year, the world was no longer the "cold, wet, miserable" motto the recon boys knew so well. Below Courthouse Bay, beaches, wadis, and hidden subdivisions inches away from the brackish water—these seaside hamlets were an aesthetic deviation from the Walmart-cultured nether realm that awaited any who departed the front gate. The place was great for lazy beach days, soaking up the sun and forgetting all the annoyances of belonging to an institution.

The area's beach-bum vibe was in stark contrast to a trinket of its history that always captured my interest. Blackbeard the Pirate: the first rock star, the weaver of theatrics and violence, the first true prelude to a future nation's utter obsession with criminals and crime, he sailed the area and terrorized its shores. Rumor was he and his bevy would lurk in the intercoastal water, waiting to see the inbound topsails of merchant ships. Once spotted, they'd tear out of the mangroves and plunder their target. This is said to be how one of the hamlets earned its name: Topsail Island. Whether entirely accurate or not, it tickled me and a few others to be a part of an amphibious fighting force in a locale that held such an esteemed hum about that very thing.

In the early spring of 2005, entire battalions were returning from their seven-month pump—cogs in the wheel of the slow and mighty monotonous OIF[47] rotations.

Guys who did their pump, coming home together. Guys from the MEU[48], at some point in their work-up, greeting these guys as all the busses rolled in to the barracks. Broke dicks, casevaced from Iraq early due to some IED, waiting to greet their old platoon with a case of beer.

It was a great time; seeing all the old faces, trading war stories, speculating who would end up where. Would it be a MEU? Pick up team leader and punch out for one more, then contact CAG[49]? Jump from Force to Dive School in Panama City to pick up a B billet, or maybe just stay with the battalion rotation and strive to build the team of choice? Amidst all this is a detail which, once announced, would get the attention of an entire unit ready to cop off some lay.

For whatever reason, women from the north and Midwest flocked to the numerous beach house bungalows, standing sturdy and ready for their occupancy. For almost a solid year, the target-rich environment had been thoroughly exploited by myself, men from my battalion, and men from other units who I'd seen in Iraq covered in the sand and dust—transformed back into their Jingos, Patriots jerseys, and cowboy hats.

Come early 2006, 2D Recon Bn had departed once again. This time I had remained behind. It was a time of extremes. I dealt with some startling sensations of loneliness, questioned my decision not to extend, and found myself working sixty hours a week in the

---

47   Operation Iraqi Freedom
48   Marine Expeditionary Unit: quick-reaction force, deployed generally via ship
49   Combat Applications Group: AKA "Delta Force," a tier one asset, and no, you don't know anyone in it

now extinct Recon Indoctrination Platoon, esoterically known as RIP—the first filter in the path of a recon hopeful.

Although this personal era had its fair share of stress and conflict, one undeniable perk was there was practically no competition at all the back-gate bars and beaches. And although there was never any real shortage, the coming of winter begat the coming of the snow birds; the densest concentration of vacationers, galvanized by that adventurous spirit we all feel when in a new place. All elements in harmony, I capitalized on this so much that when I finally left Camp Lejeune for good, I first got Blackbeard's colors tattooed on my back, signifying how much time I spent on it in that oh-so-golden age.

Some exploits, plunderings of the migratory libido, were better than others.

ONE AFTERNOON, A BUDDY and I set out for a seafood dinner. He was one of the guys who'd escaped the engulfed Humvee near the Euphrates and ran to the berm in sweat and bandages. Since then, he'd gotten a war scar to sport, and we'd gotten to know one another pretty well. We settled on a calm, two-story restaurant right on the beach. It was one of those rinky, wooden, seafarer grubberies, with driftwood decorations and old plastic crabs hung up in old netting on the walls. We sat on the balcony, overlooking the placid Atlantic. Past the sun-beaten wooden steps leading downward was a ribbon of pale white. After a short time it meshed with rich brown sand, still moist from the outbound tide. Seagulls and sanderlings hovered and hopped about the farthest reach of the surf zone as the occasional beachgoer traversed the panorama.

We chomped on calamari and talked about how his girlfriend's pussy—while anatomically similar to girls he had had in the past—felt far better.

"I mean, think about it," he said. "'Oh, she was such good pussy,' or it wasn't. It's really the same thing, it's just how you feel about it."

"I guess you're right," I said, staring at a calamari ring. "Never really thought about it that way."

Our deep-digging into the ultimate realities about an act no more complex than the corking and uncorking of a bottle was cut short by a drunk old man. He was at the counter threatening to pulverize the hostess.

"Dude, if he hits her we are going to have to do something," said my friend, dipping his calamari in the white sauce. He got a bronze star, that bastard, I thought as I looked at the burn scar on his forearm.

"He is drunk as shit," I said. He wobbled in fury when the summoned manager couldn't hide his smirk. Before long he left, though. My friend didn't have to fight a senior citizen, and we decided it a much better plan to go to the place he'd likely tied his cantankerous knot.

As the sun set, we made our way to a favorite bar of mine. About a block from the beach, this unassuming, one-story rectangle was a watering hole where I was batting 1.000.

The air was thick with smoke—standing room only in most places—while an amalgamation of figures laughed, yelled, and humped the nearest leg to the latest, watered-down club music. Darts were thrown, glasses clanked against one another, and toasts were made as women from places like Madison and Omaha undulated in what could only have been some Midwestern premating ritual, given its impetus by the temporary liberation from their workplace, the booze, and of course the hypnotic effect of the waves breaking only a few hundred feet away.

Much of the first half of the night remains a myriad of jagged memories, not completely fitting together in harmony but rather a type of jigsaw puzzle missing a few key pieces. I saw a guy I went to MCIWS[50] with. I will never forget his story about barging into a living room in Iraq.

"So you know what happened next?" he asked with a gleam in his eyes.

"Uh—no, not really?" I replied.

"You know. The same thing we always did when you and your buddies see a bunch of Iraqis hanging out in a room—ya kill 'em, of course!"

There were two other guys from my battalion at the bar, MEU guys nowhere close to deploying. One I later heard went to Valhalla, Jimi Hendrix style; the other guy, possibly the only marine allergic to beer. A solid operator, but three drinks was all it took for him to be falling over, laughing or crying, in your face or passed out by a car that vaguely resembled his own. His most recent episode at that time was he had punched out another unit's duty. This fiasco resulted in a rather hilarious formation where the beaten duty, escorted by a sergeant major who could barely pronounce his Rs, surgically scoured our ranks looking for the face of the perpetrator. Little did the duo realize that while the dipshit with the black eye had to walk around in front of an entire battalion with a big neon sign over his head, blinking "I'm a fucking pussy," the guilty party was nestled safely in some clandestine place, awaiting word that the investigation had gone cold.

---

50   Marine Combat Instructor of Water Survival

Anyway, at some point, after we all had pounded enough beer to make an operation-risk-matrix card spontaneously combust, a couple of women approached us. Both blonde, well over forty, a bit burned from what was likely a solid week of lying on the beach hungover, and sporting that invitingly obvious "I'm a stark-mad horny tourist" smile. Showing the dental enhancements paid for by their most recent divorces, their grins wrinkled the crow's feet into deep ravines, amplified by the negation of full facial expressions due to the steadfast and dutiful Botox.

What is so beautiful about moments such as these is the role reversal. In most societies where a paragraph written or typed on some piece of paper dictates it illegal to club your mate of choice on the head like a baby seal (thus whisking them off to indulge in your flagrant delight), we are socially engineered to accept, execute, and predict the male as the initiator of the ultimately sex-driven conversation. With few exceptions, any encounter witnessed by a third party will observe the male armor his ego, think of something clever and hopefully not too cliché to say, and march steadily once more into the breach to test his attributes against the vetting system of the approached female.

Anyone who has a pair of testicles and has lived in a military town will uniformly confirm that this ritual is warped and magnified exponentially due to the abnormal ratio of *poles* to *holes*. In a place like Camp Lejeune, North Carolina, it was not uncommon to see a two-hundred-pound woman being fought over by a gaggle of young marines with six-pack abs. The repercussions of such a socio-psychological arrangement were extreme, and opening the door for some behemoth, who responded to your act with the same condescension one would expect from a blonde cokehead, Hollywood runway model—well, it got old.

The seasonal crop of snow-birds was a breath of fresh air from the aforementioned social abnormality. We were a group of men who got up to run mile after mile before the rest of the civilized world had rolled out of their beds and cursed their alarm clocks. Considering the sheer amount of money spent on protein powder, coupled with the emphatic obsession with all forms of fitness, it was nice to feel that such hard work was recognized. So what if their skin was a bit leathery.

What occurred next is still debated. I was told I was cock-blocking Mr. Duty-puncher, but I distinctly recall trying to set him up with a MILF in apex heat. Be that as it may, at some point the two women dragged me and the accuser of my alleged cock-block antics onto the dance floor.

It was a slow song—a sensual, subtle tune to kick off the romantic acts that would ensue. She French kissed me between puffs of her Pall Mall. Grabbing my ass with one hand, high-fiving her friend with the other, my date and her friend celebrated their joint conquest of two males with no facial hair and hard bodies who would most certainly not need the blue pill. As their hands clapped in unified joy, their cigarettes sparkled and flamed—short-lived fireworks signifying, well, everything.

By the fourth or fifth song I could barely stand. She had pumped so much booze in me that I was going nowhere but where she wanted. I must have looked like John Harker in Bram Stoker's *Dracula*—deficient in gross motor movement while being sucked on by a being possessing a vagina. Instead of blood, vodka ran down my neck as her kisses became more slovenly and proprietary. The thing I remember most was at this point, as she slung me against her like someone moving a crash-test dummy from one car to the next, I locked eyes with a row of wallflowers. Cute girls, my age, with perky bee-stung lips, dressed to impress—and completely ignored by all the marines in the bar. There were more over-forties in the place, and all meaning business. The snow-birds had swooped in and collected a marine apiece and were not about to let go now.

This was the beautiful thing about most marines and, I'd learn later, most door-kickers of the ground combat world: you could shove your expectations right up your own ass. We would plow something tight and moist regardless, and any entitlement to some weak form of courtship was exactly where it needed to be—on the dance floor getting kicked to death by the feet of people about to fuck, and drowning in the sweat and spilled beer of the same.

The lights turned on. The hour had apparently come.

"Barrrrs closed!" yelled some girl with a thick southern accent.

My date told me she had a place nearby and I was to accompany her. Indeed. It was when she had me get into an SUV with another couple that questions began to arise. No worries, she quickly explained, they were her sister and brother-in-law. Although I was spinning slightly, when I focused on them strong enough, their inherent discomfort with the whole ordeal was chiseled into their faces. I got the impression they weren't the least bit surprised I was in their backseat.

Barely able to speak, I do remember them asking me how old I was. I was twenty-three. "I'm—twenty—twenty-six," I cleverly replied. My date laughed and told me she was forty-six. She was twice my age. My mind tried to fixate on the weird math, but was soon distracted. She rewarded my answer with a huge open-mouthed face sucking, where this time I felt the faint cracks around her lips, resembling a flexible and articulate asshole, which of course were due to all the years of smoking.

After a short drive we arrived at their beach cabin. She and I made our way to a screened-in porch. We smoked some. I unfortunately remember doing something involving her foot and my tongue. I'm positive she asked me some questions about being in the Marine Corps, warm with a spectator's amazement that doesn't exist in those within even remote proximity of a military base.

The final Pall Mall snuffed out on the nearest board, she took to her feet. It was time. Now, I'm not too sure about what their sleeping arrangements were prior to my stumbling arrival, but the woman escorted me into a small bedroom where a sleeping teenage girl lay on a twin bed. The moistened harpy demanded the mattress, and damn right. I locked eyes with this girl, her super-groggy and I ultra-lit. She was brunette, maybe eighteen, and her innocent, sleek look made me think of a figure skater. Her aunt told her to go sleep on the couch.

It was chaos in the threshold of the doorway. The evicted teen tried to skirt past me, but my hyper-masculine proclivities fueled me to grab her by her arm and pull her back into the room. She fought her way to abstinent freedom, shrugging out of my grip and egressing with a rumpled PJ top. The last thing I recalled before the door shut was watching her walk into the living room, where the growing audible discomfort was rumbling from the other family members, too mortified to sleep.

The door slammed shut, and my attention was ripped back into the room by the two brown hands pulling at my collar.

The headboard would not stop banging. Even in my drunken state I still couldn't help but feel the childhood-ending impose, imagining an entire family listening to that rhythmic and consistent, crisp smack. I was too drunk to finish, and finally laid on my edge of the confiscated cot to pass out.

What felt like one minute later, I was awoken by pale morning blue penetrating the wooden mini blinds. The air had that morning beach smell and viscosity to it—almost extra salty and somehow bleeding through the walls. Turning her onto her stomach, I jammed a finger in her ass, creating a moan that was half sexual and half from the supernal depths of infinite, spiritual agony. Going fifth gear doggy style, the headboard resumed its duty, much like a merry dog convinced of its job to bark when the doorbell rings. Needing to get back to base, I finished in record time, unloading into her and beginning the search for my jeans.

For years I wondered what blonde mongoloid I produced via what was almost certainly one of the last of her eggs. I got a random email once from someone with the subject "I hope you like these." In the body of the message were several pictures of a toe-head boy, strikingly similar to pictures of me at the Child Development Center in the mid-eighties. I quickly deleted the message and remain confident with reasonable certainty I never gave her my email address.

Tiptoeing out into the living room, I was met with the uncomfortable stare of the guy who'd driven the SUV. In the softness of morning I could see he was short and thin with a brown seventies porn star mustache. He stood with the irked grimace of a man who spent the night prior listening to his sister-in-law get pounded while moaning like some oceanic mammal, yet in full realization that the unwanted pounder would likely feed him his teeth and then run a hand up his daughter's back if he dared interfere. He had the task of now pouring breakfast cereal for the several children that had been in rooms unseen. Just pour the cereal. Don't look him in the eyes. Things are normal, kids, things are totally, totally fine. Aunt Carpe Noctem is on vacation too, and if we all pray together her *new friend* will be leaving soon.

"There are just some things you don't want to know," sighed the teenage girl to her mom. At the tail of the sigh was a hard giggle.

"Uhm—I don't know where I am, and I, uhm—I need to get home."

Dad pointed toward the cardinal direction that housed the marines, the leathernecks, a group I'm certain that family never looked at the same again. I quickly, without looking up, made my way to the front door and out of the house. Stepping out into the thick dew of morning, I breathed in the sea salt and gathered my bearings. As my eyes strained to make out the thin black asphalt that would take me northbound and home, I heard the porch door open.

"Bye," sang the snow-bird to my back, out from her confines of the screen and wooden cage.

Soon on my trek home, a day-shift cop, fresh on the beat with his first cup of coffee in the console, stopped me. I saw his high and tight, with the side of his head so polished you could read a credit card number off the reflective surface.

At the police station, I was harassed and harangued that a recon marine was "left behind" by his buddies—yet again, somehow destroying the archaic and myopic slogans the Marine Corps is immortal for. I didn't tell them I ditched my buddies to fill up a vacationer older than their field supervisor; instead, I shook my head, laughed, and had them call me a cab.

12

THE BRIDGE REP

SPRING 2004

ETTING INTO THE SOF[51] community in general has always been, and likely always will be, a righteous kick to the dick. Arguments will always abound as to whether BUDS[52] is harder than the PJ[53] pipeline, or if Ranger school is harder than BUDS and/or ARS, or whose sniper school is harder (therefore qualitatively better), or of course whether Marine Recon is actually SOF or just good dudes who went to the wrong recruiting office. I have come to bracket a lot of those esoteric arguments, and there are certainly a number of legitimate issues to support or damage a lot of the claims. One thing is for sure, though: very few SOF operators have gone through more than one MOS-producing school. The knowledge of one school is hard to compare with another, considering one was firsthand, leaving their sweat and name attached to that school forever, compared to the secondhand nature of learning the finer details of the other schools. With that in mind, and with years of postmilitary SOF friendship building, it seems the design on the

---

51   Special Operations Forces: this encompasses all Spec Ops in the US military; intent on employing and training the smartest, strongest, and toughest individuals to complete difficult missions under the harshest conditions
52   Basic Underwater Demolition School; where Navy SEALS are born/made
53   Air Force Pararescue

hoodie eventually means less and less, and the gut check itself, in its roughest intrinsic form, produces men of a very similar mind-set.

For me and my brethren, ARS was the big filter. Broken into three phases—Land Navigation, Patrolling, and Amphibious—the days and weeks were generally dictated by extreme amounts of daily physical training followed by classroom and field instruction with regards to the particular phase we were in.

Patrolling, the largest phase, contained a special week that we had been preparing for since RIP. A student was likely to experience several days in a row without so much as a minute of sleep, little food, and full combat-load movements in the steep terrain of Fort A.P. Hill. Also, it was rumored that if a tactical error was made to a certain, loosely-defined degree, we would be subject to instantaneous CS gassing.

Patrol Week in Fort A.P. Hill was an event that required the whole of you, nothing less. The entire class had already been operating in small six- to eight-man teams since week one. As people dropped, and they did, the teams got smaller and occasionally had to be slightly reformulated. Bussed from Fort Story to A.P. Hill, those who remained knew a significant, maybe the most significant, course challenge was at hand. After a quick terrain walk and a final land navigation exercise, Patrol Week arrived.

The inner-team billets were to change every twenty-four hours, as a mission ended (whether success or failure) and another began. A guy who had survived ARS up until then as a tight-lipped gray man, who hadn't even chimed in once about how the chow was at Little Creek, would all at once be bequeathed the role of team leader. And then, of course, the opposite was in full effect: some grunt from the fleet or some marine officer with years of time in service would then be positioned to take instant and obedient orders from a PFC[54] who had just celebrated his first anniversary in the Marine Corps. Couple those changes with increasing fatigue, and interesting results were bound to happen.

My team consisted of eight men, mostly guys I had gone through RIP with; in addition, a grunt with about three years of fleet time, a reservist from Montana, and a captain with decadent tattoos circling his thighs.

Every team would have at least one instructor, or *walker*, who came along on the patrol. The walker was the evaluator of the team. He carefully watched and critiqued the students' individual actions, relative to their billet during the mission. He was also the administrator of discipline, the final arbitrator, via what seemed to be a limitless supply of CS gas.

A quick note on CS gas: O-chlorobenzylidene malononitrile, used most commonly for riot control around the world, is a volatile solvent that irritates the eyes, sinuses, and lungs ferociously. When the milky, faintly yellow cloud disperses into the air, it inexplicably wafts toward the human, who is either running the other way or scrambling to don a gas mask (or both, in my case). Come across this and you will never forget it. The itch in the eyes feels more like a product of pathology than some chemical reaction. Even the slightest inhale will cause the top quarter of both lungs to burn and result in a rapid fire of shallow coughs. Most significant, however, is the reaction the sinuses have. That acrid unique odor—it crawls into your nasal cavities like a Nam-era tunnel rat. Clinging to every nose hair and cilia and then all at once attacking every inner realm existing above the Adam's apple, you explode—a snot bomb. Someone completely naive to such an experience would not believe the human body capable of such instantaneous fluid production. Honestly, it's a great way

---

54   Private first class: E-2

to clear up clogged sinuses, and as someone who had habitually suffered from said effect since my late teens, surviving a blitzkrieg of CS would allow for some very comfortable, almost elated breathing afterward.

The hour arrived, so the missions came.

By day five, every team was pretty smoked. In total, we had been allotted, I think, around three and a half hours of sleep for that entire week and had conducted four complete missions, all requiring extensive movement. Of all the missions that teams were responsible for conducting, the "bridge report" was rumored to be the most difficult.

A quick note on reporting: Stemming from the Cold War era, the Reconnaissance community was generally expected to operate as an information-gathering tool, conveyed to the appropriate higher personnel via NATO report formats. A red-covered manual containing specific, line-by-line instructions covered pretty much everything imaginable: road, river, landing zone, etc.

Bridges have been the target of military defense, engineering, and demolition as long as they have been around. It is no great stretch of the imagination as to why Robert Jordan was tasked with destroying one in Hemingway's *For Whom the Bell Tolls*. The bridge report, or bridge rep, was like all the other missions: get there in a tactical, clandestine manner; conduct an efficient reconnaissance of the objective; leave objective; and successfully move to extract. Sounds easy enough when read from the comfort of a couch or recliner, but executing this is another story altogether.

What made the bridge rep particularly challenging was the distance from insert to objective. The team that had gone before us leaked that if we skirted a small river, represented on our maps, it would take us directly to the bridge. Now, normally such a linear danger area would be an immediate no-go, but it was confirmed that the CO[55] of the school walked with that team the entire mission and had no problem with the route, so we figured *what the hell.*

As the sun was setting, all teams rucked up and stepped off.

Into the tree line we were absorbed.

We were immediately gassed. Instructor discretion was apparently paramount, and our walker was in no mood to tolerate a simple route. Within the first hour we had been forcibly augmented from our original route to an extent that our team leader, delirious, had trouble figuring out where we were. I was billeted the assistant team leader (ATL), picking up the rear, and wasn't doing that bad, considering the circumstances. Recalling the intense elevation and relief (dictated on the map as thin lines, whose proximity to the other indicates the steepness of both incline and decline of terrain) to the west of our planned route, I realized quickly how far west we had deviated as I watched my team ascend the first thick, deciduous hillside.

Until about 4:00 a.m., what transpired was a series of: up, down, gas, repeat. At one point, something entirely unexpected occurred. Climbing a hill in the blackness, our team had linked up with several other teams. We were now a platoon-size movement, bursting through the brush. Some of my favorite hard-hitters were there, particularly two guys close to me. One, powerfully built, shaved head, and with a penchant for articulate hatred, left the insurance industry after 9/11 to do nothing less than go to war. The other guy, equally formidable in stature, was a nail bomb of confrontation. When not telling off some lifer or frustrating a platoon mate, he could be found merrily lip syncing to top forty ballads. He never drank, never used tobacco, and dressed like a Hooters waitress in the various gyms we all

_____

55   Commanding officer

swarmed together. His inexplicable obsession with ultra-pop divas like Kelly Clarkson was soon forgotten when he would do such things as blowing the neck out of an Iraqi kid with a heavy gun. This duo's collective loathing for religion (usually taking it on the chin was Christianity) was something they were bizarrely vocal about when around the other. This fact was not lost on me, and in my exhaustion this colocation in the woods felt akin to the four horsemen of the apocalypse—gathering, and just waiting on Petulance to round the bend. They had suffered the beaver dams as well, and now we were fuckin' invincible.

Of course, this was merely a hallucination (an extremely common reaction to extended exertion with little to no sleep), and I was pulled from it when the team came to an abrupt halt. Our team leader, taken over by hallucinogenic exhaustion, had wandered up to his neck in brutally cold water. Maybe it was some brand new form of a "leader's recon," or maybe the mother ship was calling him back up, but his hypothermic tarriance resulted in the removal of his team leader responsibilities. Nestled somewhere in the back, between two guys just a little less tired and a little more warm, he resumed the march as I was tapped as the new TL.

I got us pretty darn close, I must say. I think it was somewhere during a brief map check, sticking my head out from under the poncho liner to see the CS come tumbling in—cumbersome, slow, and obnoxious—that we uniformly said, "Fuck it."

All members of the team got a failing grade that night, but I came to find out that I got one of the highest failing grades.

Though not particularly a tale of chest-beating triumph or conquest, it was absolutely real. Very few people went through Patrol Week without failing at least one patrol; we had ours, and it was dismal. A few days later we would participate in the final patrol, and then in a race involving distance, water, and of course CS gas. Our team came in second, and I remember the hilarious group showers afterward: cammie paint etched into the crow's feet of faces too euphoric to fully realize their exhaustion. Two men were next to me, laughing like drunk lunatics. One would die a master sergeant in Afghanistan; the other would have a litter of kids and go work for the FBI. Stacked boxes of cold pizza awaited us outside the showers, and the Recon MOS awaited us a few short weeks after.

13

GET THE FUCK BACK IN
THE BARRACKS

SUMMER 2005

S OUTHEASTERN SKIES TURN FROM bruise to a great gray. The air seems lighter than normal and you can taste the electricity. Bandit gusts of wind rile up some nearby treetops and vanish just as suddenly as they appeared. The base is literally sold out of beer, and the crisp sound of one opening is heard as an excited voice says, "This is gonna be the shit."

The hurricane season had come to Camp Lejeune. No one is completely certain as to why, but the Marine Corps has a strange fascination with preparation for natural disasters. The most likely reason is because it is a way for particular higher-ups to push many of the same buttons as seen in war. Sandbags, water sources, personal protective equipment, communication, and accountability—all present and without even having to sweat it out at a CAX[56]. The hilarious overkill is undeniably countered by the ravenous appetite for booze and mischief that goes on within the base as the rain pours. This schizophrenia was seen very clearly at Courthouse Bay, 2005.

The Marine Corps' catch-all for safety, the flak jacket and Kevlar helmet, was ordered to be worn by all marines on base who would be leaving their barracks room for any reason. If you were

---

getting your laundry, you had better be kitted up and ready for anything. If you had to run through the storm to your car, they had better see the splatter of rain bouncing off your fastened helmet.

Not a single flack or Kevlar was seen in the barracks of my battalion, lest in a moment of jest, and usually the only thing on. A wobbling cock and white ass chasing some drunk down the catwalk, and in full battle rattle.

The base had placed a water bull in the rear of our barracks. The "water bull," for those who have never seen such a thing, is merely a large tank of water affixed to a trailer body. Holding around four hundred gallons meant for drinking, these are placed in training areas when personnel are to be out in the field for a bit—or at a barracks where the pipe-given water source may be compromised.

By the time I had made my way out back, one person swam in it and another was pissing down into a four-hundred-gallon toilet.

Every bit of hyper-precautious Marine Corps defiled, the hurricane party was in full swing. The wind and rain had come. A few guys in bright-colored thongs, strutting by with beer in hand, as random fireworks would explode, hurled from the top deck of the barracks. Most of the focus was on two guys, one who'd donated all the clothes for Boot Night, and the other Dez, from my team. They were both trying to use 550 cord and a poncho liner to take flight.

The first guy looked like something out of a sci-fi B-movie you see at 3:00 a.m. This brave space cadet was wearing a racing helmet, full wet suit, and Rollerblades. He had rigged his poncho liner to open in front of him, attached to the 550 cord leash he had made.

Dez was in a pair of shorts and standard greenside deuce gear (combat-grade belt and suspenders with an assortment of pouches).

He had tied his poncho liner, via 550 cord as well, to key points on his belt and suspenders. We were all pretty fixed on him, waiting to see exactly what would happen when a forceful gust took hold.

From my left peripheral, I saw two guys running toward the woods in gas masks, disappearing in the sheets of rain.

It was at this point we all noticed a lone Humvee slowly making its way toward our barracks.

If it is possible to detect the rage of a vehicle's passenger by the stalking velocity of its approach, followed by its sudden oblong parking job, it was confirmed here. Out marched what we later found out to be the Division OOD[57]. He was in so much rain-protective gear you could barely make out the flak and Kevlar. As he high-stepped toward our barracks, his scowl could be seen through the billowing contents of our most enjoyed meteorological phenomenon. Trailing behind him we could make out his driver—a short, squatty Mexican kid who was well aware of the façade he had to uphold until the duty changeover (which had to have felt like it was never going to come). This OOD, likely a young captain, was in no mood for games. It was his watch and by God it was his ass if one of the thousands of stewed marines happened to get hurt. The thong-wearers scattered. He zeroed his attention in on Dez. As luck would have it, a gust of wind inflated his poncho liner at that very moment. Our man Dez looked like a semipro body builder, so the best the wind could do was lift him off his feet just long enough to put him on his ass.

---

57   Officer of the day

Poncho liner still full and being pushed, he skipped and skidded right to the feet of the furious OOD.

"Get the fuck back in the barracks!" the OOD screamed. "We are in a category one hurricane!" The OOD and his obliged sidekick turned around to return to their Humvee.

So many things crossed my mind at that moment: my beer was empty, a category one wasn't shit where I came from, and what was going through the fuming OOD's head as he turned to see our other poncho parasailer, dangerously flying down the street on a pair of Rollerblades, pulled by a fully inflated poncho liner?

It was then that the grand harassment began. A chorus of insults, hurled fireworks, and a "go back to Quantico" made their way through the diminishing rainfall. It was like watching some invading army retreat. As the Humvee left, morale exploded. Our spirits were off the charts, and we needed more.

Some of us decided to go to Onslow Beach, the beach connected with the base that was not more than a few minutes by vehicle. About nine of us piled into a couple of cars and made our way to the surging coast. Our group did not run into any interference—no roving Humvees or rain-soaked MPs[58] dashing madly toward our unauthorized presence. All was well until we reached the one bridge that we had to cross. Cliché and classic, a wall of sandbags blocked our approach to the churning and chaotic beach, almost within our eager grasp.

A moment was taken to inventory the situation, then the drivers parked the cars on the shoulder. The wall was scaled, and the beach was ours.

The winds whipped clothing around bodies, hurled sand like tiny needles, and guided in the monster waves. The hurricane was dying, but its slow death rattle held a lingering rage just enough.

---

58   Military Police

We were still in one. Professional surfers would have fought tooth and nail to be standing on this beach, this day. Laughter and smiles that can only belong to the young man, invulnerable and bolstered by his pack, some ran along the beach like human kites while others took to the water. Within the group was Derrick, Dez, a man I'd see at a shooting course years later, one who would survive a gunshot wound to the head in Afghanistan, and another who would succumb to burn injuries received in Iraq.

That day I was one of those in the surf. The waves were literally pulling the flooring off the sandy bottom. Clumps of shells and crustaceans pounded down on the bodysurfers, almost twenty feet high just a moment before and now rolling in the tumult. Despite what was certainly dangerous, those out in the water would always emerge, unbeaten or damn close to it—a boyish freedom impossible to replicate.

Pictures taken and with a big middle finger to the powers that wished to contain our energy, we returned to the barracks. A day or so later, the sandbags and tainted water bulls disappeared, garrison life resumed, and our group soon returned to a placid, tranquil beach—a timid mimic of a vivid, wilder version.

14

EXISTENTIALIST NIGHTMARE AND WRITINGS FROM IRAQ

Our unit had two companies of recon marines. Bravo Company (B Co.) was considered on paper to be the battalion's "main effort." Usually closer in proximity to the city of Fallujah, B Co. was clean, upwardly mobile, and a shiny stark contrast to my alma mater, Alpha Company (A Co.).

One night, in TQ[59], I dreamt that I was participating in a triathlon. It wasn't a normal one, though; it had all these obstacle courses and fun houses involved, and a bunch of porn stars were running in it. Some busty blonde and I were neck and neck going through this fun house. We were going up and down the stairs elbowing one another, fighting for the lead. You could cut the tension with a knife as the voluptuous vixen and I fought for glory. Suddenly, I was detoured. Some brunette was bent over a table in chains and leather, just waiting for me. *Fuck the race!* I must have thought because I went into the room and started performing analingus on her. We chatted a bit as I tongued her ass. I could taste shit, but I didn't care. I slipped it in and started having anal sex with my eyes shut. As I fucked, I started to hear a distinct metallic clicking noise.

I opened my eyes to realize that I was no longer with a girl, but was now bound in a wooden chair in front of a table. A harsh

---

Al Taqaddum Airbase, an airbase in central Iraq

light lurched forward from the tabletop, shining in my face. There were three men who looked to be KGB or something, one holding a curved blade up to his throat, smiling. Another had a pistol and was pulling the hammer back and then riding the trigger home. They were all smiling as the hammer kept getting recocked over and over.

I woke up to see my team leader next to my cot. In the weaver stance, he was practicing pistol drills. He glanced down at me as I stared at him, confused and with a headache from dehydration.

A Co., in the mid-section of the 2000s, was arguably the most sordid carnival heap to ever work under a military standard. In Camp Fallujah, stately B Co. Marines would walk through A Co. trailers, holding tight security as hoots and hisses emitted from the darkened windows and vague crannies. Piss bottles hurled at Bravo heads, they knew if they stopped they would likely be mugged and have their gear traded for DVDs.

Listening to half the platoon in their Cretan drunkenness. Henry Miller, well I really think I am missing something he's trying to say. One thing his writing has made me do lately is appreciate the hidden beauty in all things, mostly hidden in things that are looked down upon. To see ruby and gold in the blood from a guy's forehead after a fistfight. Tequila brings out aggression and it impresses me how brotherly all the A2[60] guys are, even though we're all stressed and want to get back to the States. The beauty in all things! Americans are so brainwashed to see "beauty" only in things of force-fed value or sex appeal. If you live your life through that scope, I think you'll never see what beauty is. I still can't really label it. I suppose it's a quality in something that makes you feel good about either it or yourself. To see beauty in two

---

60   Alpha Two: the platoon I operated in while deployed to Iraq; there were three platoons in Alpha Company: A1, A2, and A3

smashed marines bitching about life and how in the civilian world they'd never hang out together, while the whole time one's arm is around the other.

B Co. guys would be doing mag changes in their room at 9:00 p.m. on a Friday night, while most of A Co. would be convoying out the back gate to bum rush the front door of our favorite strip club. B Co. guys were the ones going into the offices to talk about reenlistment; A Co. Marines had become legends for beating the piss out of a dozen engineer students and then, briefly, escaping from the MP's car. Somehow, despite the highest DUI rate per capita in the Division, we received the Division Safety Award right before going wheels up to participate in Operation Iraqi Freedom.

We've been in the camp three days. We spent a full day flying and one in Kuwait. We moved to TQ north of Fallujah for a couple more days. The majority of this place is a barren wasteland, sheer nothingness but wind and sand. I'd hate to live here! The camp is awesome: trailers, chow halls, gym, phone center, showers (although cold), etc. It's a fucking desert Hilton. Last night while we were on the BZO[61] range, on the outskirts of the camp two mortars came in and killed the oncoming regimental XO[62] and comm officer and seriously wounded the sergeant major. The good food and air-conditioning doesn't hide the fact that we are not safe here and these people want to kill us. We are ordered not to tell our family and friends anything about what we are doing. That bugs me; I like to inform my parents. The brutal truth of things is often more solace than sugarcoated lies or silence. I agree with it, though; it is for our own security.

---

61   Battle sight zero: adjusting sights of a weapon to obtain accuracy; as per the individual shooter
62   Executive officer

Due to an ill-planned parking job, an entire stock of B Co. vehicles were roasted by a single mortar, launched by an Iraqi who must have gone to bed that night certain Allah had rewarded his mortar-tube marksmanship with a glorious fire. Of course, this same platoon was soon given all the vehicles from an A Co. platoon. Destined to walk the Zaidon with bloused boots and a clean shave, A Co. Marines penchant for theft developed early. By the time all vehicles were returned to our company, it had become SOP: Vehicles stop to set up a forward operating base. Nearest house is pillaged; pillows, blankets, the occasional Koran and family photo. One hard-charger would seed panties found in temporarily confiscated drawers. Violence erupted in our AO[63] and the pass times took a backseat to a lot of long hours and a bit of bloodshed.

I've seen the machine come alive! You dwell in it so deeply at times that you forget you're a part of it. I doubt a gear in a clock knows it's a gear in a clock after long enough, especially if the clock is not in motion. In spite of the fact that the parts are made of bitching, nagging flesh, the machine works. The machine is iron. A standing, manlike iron shape thats crushing hand oozes liquid metal as it makes a sudden but strategic clasp. Sparks fly and no expression is made. In darkness, it stands a giant among giants.

Three A Co. operators sit in a stripper's car, the front passenger door flung open. Two strippers roll on the ground outside a trailer, like cats, with an assortment of hair-care products strewn about on the flattened grass. Fighting over one of the guys in the backseat, the owner of the car had seen her bathroom contents being tossed out by the other one, perched on the center-block stoop of the trailer just a moment before. Now engaged in hair-pulling combat. A

63   Area of operations

matriarchal crone, equipped in a Johnny Cash shirt and a frog voice, attempts to break up the scrap.

"Steal her car, dude," from the backseat.

"I am not stealing a fucking stripper's shit-box car. Okay, shut up, here she comes."

Dispute resolution complete, the four make it back to the base. The victor fucks her trophy on his bed, blades of grass all over the sheets. Her phone is thrown in the barracks pond for not being receptive to group sex.

I woke up in the same position I usually sleep in, my right side against the trailer wall. It was dark and I felt...odd. There was a window-size gate right above my right shoulder, parallel to the window in the middle of the wall. It was open and one side was being moved to and fro by the wind. I knew immediately I had made a mistake. How stupid could I have been to forget to shut and lock it?! There was something there, I couldn't actually see it; the world was black and so was it. I could only be aware of its presence. I was in trouble and I experienced for the first time what it is to be "frozen stiff" by fear. I couldn't move, as if I had two bodies, one inside the other. The inner one would respond to my mind, pulling and tugging on the reluctant limbs of my outer shell. I lay there, watching the creature caress my chest with what I thought was an arm. Although my flesh and nerves couldn't detect it, a cold feeling appeared along with a sense of violation.

A provocative whistle turned their heads, all three of them. In a mad dash, dust and leaves awhirl; it was like a video was put on fast forward of marines running into their rooms to avoid standing at Attention for Colors. The three female Second lieutenants made their approach. The cat call; they

were having none of it. Looking to my left, then to my right,
I am the only person now on the entire first deck. In their
crosshairs; I, woefully late, retreat into my room. One of
the few A Co. Marines to defy our unwashed and decadent
aura was the very one to go all David Lee Roth on these
girls with a beach voyeur's whistle, and then vanish—but it
was my door they approached. The door gets knocked. The
confrontation begins. The confrontation ends. I am reported.
I am yelled at. I go on leave that same day, and refuse to
pick up the beer cans one of the lieutenants demanded upon
their unsaluted departure. Upon return from leave comes the
official reprimand. In my room, platoon mates bring over a
case of beer. I push aside a paperback copy of *In Search of
the Warrior Spirit.* The case finds a home.

I read. Shit, books are just mnemonic devices anyway. I never
read to fulfill a need to look or even be intellectual. I really don't
even read to entertain myself. I read to answer questions, period.
Think about it; learn all that you want to know. Books are created
by man and read by man, an intellectual cannibalism that feeds on
itself. I read to find answers, I live to find answers.

15

B.A.H.

"The 'humor' expressed on this page and similar pages...contribute to a culture that permits and seems to encourage sexual assault and abuse...many of the pictures imply women only advance professionally by performing sexual favors and otherwise promote the idea that women are inferior and only useful as sexual objects and sandwich makers."

—California State Representative Jackie Speier in a letter to the secretary of defense, commandant of the Marine Corps, and various others regarding a particularly raw military subculture Facebook page

"Politics and an open-minded scientific discussion of human nature mix about as well as oil and water."

—Michael Ghiglieri, *The Dark Side of Man*

FALL 2005

THERE'S THE DISTINCT POSSIBILITY that a bizarre yet primitive nature is brought out when in certain institutions. For instance, while I was in Iraq, word had gotten out that a female lieutenant had been the willing centerpiece of a gang bang. According to certain people, who'll remain in the shadows, she was blonde, short, and sturdy with hips ready to pop out a couple dependents. During this poly-coitus she wore a gas mask, and the climactic moment of this extreme case of fraternization was the insertion of an M16A2's compensator up her ass.

The story has always resonated with me due to the high number of reported sexual assault cases in the military. Supposing a few years later, after a ring on the finger and some time to deliberate, the gang bang centerpiece speaks about her experience with disdain and remorse, what are we to make of it? There's no question that a willing participant isn't the same as someone who has an act forced upon them. However, despite the machine-gun scream of rape culture, and the urge to assume defilement after defilement is swept under the rug by the raging hard-on of a cleaner for the Good Ol' Boys Club, most who've served in the military will attest the unpopular and politically-targeted view that too many cases that go raging up the flagpole actually commenced in a nature similar to that of the libidinous lieutenant.

Sex and military life are systematically untraditional. Paper marriages for BAH[64] and the UCMJ's[65] definition of "sodomy" are only the tip of a cum-soaked iceberg—floating in a freezing sea of loneliness, hyper-masculinity, government checks, childlike invulnerability, and evolutionary psychology.

This all can be placed into two apt categories actually, and once done, one can't help but reflect on their differences. The sexual exploits of servicemen back home are nothing compared to what happens overseas. CONUS, the extent of it usually involves a cheater or some sloppy parody of European porn in a barracks room. OCONUS, however, a compensator up a lieutenant's ass only paints a tame and timid teaser for what has transpired in

64   Basic allowance for housing: a significant financial and lifestyle perk, and incentive to get married while in the military; also the primary food source for the Dependapotamus
65   Uniform code of military justice; the authority in military law and regulation

ports, forward operating bases, and huts of conquered villages as long as such have existed. Strip off the veneer; moral, immoral, or amoral, sexuality is a central theme reoccurring in the lives of men with guns in a foreign land.

When I was contracting in Afghanistan, I ran into one of the most unsavory human chancres in all my life. A legend of sorts, this sordid debauchee was every type of foulness encapsulated on two legs. With thick-glasses, bristly white chin hair, and a personality as charming as a tapeworm—having contracted for several years, and feeling the horny imps of below start to nibble on his feet, he left the gun world to enjoy retirement in Vietnam. His plan was widely known, and thanks to the few who kept in touch with him, the plan was apparently executed.

He bought a bushel of twelve-year-old girls, maybe boys too. He spent the remainder of his days—which couldn't have been many—lying on his side, smoking cigarettes, and watching Vietnamese television. According to those who knew his fetishes, as he lifted one leg like a dog airing itself in front of a fan, the human chattel were subjugated to licking his asshole and sucking on his nut sack. Maybe most amazing of all, the sex slaves were Buddhists, and you can't help but wonder if they contemplated what they did in their former lives to deserve their current occupation.

And then, of course, there are my contributions to this library of acts and testimonies which encompass cum and the gun, albeit devoid of underage harems, and mostly all taking place on native soil. To wit:

BILLY WAS A SHORT, uppity New Jersey native. In uniform he looked like, and sometimes was, the guy who'd start the most shit at the wrong times. In regular clothes, he sort of resembled a clean-cut version of Jackass's "Party Boy." Billy would always leave our barracks Friday evening, dressed to the nines with a pep in his step. While many of us geared up for our pilgrimage to the strip club out the back gate, case of Bud Light sweating on the catwalk, Billy would pull out from the barracks parking lot, checking his teeth in the mirror. After a couple days of our gym routines, beer, and Xbox, we'd see him return Sunday night.

One day I finally had to ask, "Bill, where the fuck you going?"

"If I tell you, you gotta promise not to let it get out," he said with a furrowed brow.

"Yeah man, sure."

The next three minutes would forever alter, and formally shape, my sex life. One must remember this was before Tinder, Bumble, I'm-not-looking-for-a-one-nighter-but-I-have-nothing-but-cleavage-selfies apps—all of that mess. I learned of a website teeming with horny women. Cheaters, divorcees, cougars, MILFs, dangerously curious college girls, and oddities so on the fringe they couldn't be classified.

This was great news! One rather frustrating detail of living in Camp Lejeune was that it was an entire county full of men. Sure, you had your occasional female marine, spit bottle in hand, or the repugnant monstrosities out in town, but even with a lenient head count, men still overwhelmingly outnumbered women in the 28542 zip code.

This website offered access to girls in Charlotte, Raleigh, and sometimes even Virginia Beach if the profile lassoed the phallus sufficiently enough.

I was on it immediately; posted two shirtless pictures taken by Dez and on the hunt. The cornucopia was overwhelming. The spectrum galactic. In one moment a picture of a three-hundred-pound woman, unshaved and spread eagle, then right next to her an up-from-under shot of a sleek stripper in librarian glasses blowing a kiss—blowing me a kiss. It took me a bit to learn the cosmetics of the site, and I also learned fast the futility of lengthy, individual messages. A canned email polished up and a quaint intro later, I was soon making contact.

The first target I had any real correspondence with was a tight-jeaned Southern belle, fiery and fresh off a nasty divorce. "Come fuck me tonight" was her message, more direct than a platoon sergeant. I touched myself involuntarily, followed by wailing in despair as I realized I could not fulfill her request. Alas, the Marine Corps dictated some god-awful schedule, and to my heartache I had to decline. Soon after, however, I received a thoughtful message from a five-foot-two brunette with a tiny waist and a sun tattooed around her belly button.

She commented on how I put off an artistic essence—and damn right. Finally, someone saw it right. And it just so happened she was sexy as hell. After a dinner with a team member, cut short by her anticipated "I'm ready" text, I was sliding my truck sideways into the parking lot of the town movie theater.

I'd never met a girl off the Internet before—hell, barely understood email—and this stranger was in the running for the hottest thing I'd ever had the chance of bedding down. Trying my best not to pace around like a caged animal, I hung out against the wall of the entrance and scanned the gaggle for *the girl in the profile pics.*

"There you are," a spritely voice said to my right. A tanned, toned beauty in tight jeans with a pearly-white smile approached me with arms outstretched. As her hug widened I saw the sun on her stomach. "I was waiting for you over there." This was possibly the most positive first encounter I'd ever had with a prospective female at the time. Something about having met online made it extra adventurous. She and I were in cahoots, some whisper draped in sexuality. We were both excited, and we both knew it.

After some movie, thoroughly upstaged by the up-down caressing of her fingers on my arm, we made our way to a dark, vacant playground. We sat in the same swing and struggled to find something to talk about. Afterward we headed to the beach, where we had sex in the sandy dark.

———◦———

FOR DAYS AFTERWARD I was floating on a cloud, a sex-cloud whose golden staircase was a mouse-click away. My poor brothers endured the flogging of my story over and over again. They were happy for me, of course, and I'm sure a few slinked off to make accounts of their own. I wanted more, and to my delight I soon got an invite from her to a quiet get-together that coming weekend at her friend's house.

The week's running on tank trails and weapons cleaning slogged until its Friday death, upon which Billy and I peeled out of the barracks parking lot, checking our teeth in our mirrors.

Following my MapQuest printout, I ended my trek in the driveway of a small family home right outside the front gate. And there she was, running up to me for another hug. She had golden makeup around her eyes, coming out the sides in that feline type of slash that strippers and Goth girls love to sport. I noticed wrinkles in her face, things I hadn't seen last time, and a smile that didn't include her eyes. No bother, it all disappeared the moment she reached down and cupped my manhood. "Take your clothes off, right now," she said in my ear. She took me by the hand, escorted me into the house, and introduced me to her friend and her friend's man.

Her friend was a bawdy redhead. She was of that uppity Irish essence, with an ass that looked to be forged from riding horseback and marine. Next to her was her man, about 130 pounds soaking wet with spacey eyes, a black high and tight, and a look that appeared to be something akin to shame. With a large, deep scar running down the right side of his head, he looked like what he was: someone who'd relatively recently just barely survived an IED attack.

"What's up, man?" I extended with a handshake. "Thanks for having me over."

He paused and looked at his girl. "No problem."

"You just get back?" I found myself asking—sort of the standard icebreaker in those areas and times, knowing wholeheartedly nobody really gave a shit either way.

"Yeah, you?"

"A few months ago. Happy to be back, around Fallujah got boring as fuck after Phantom Fury."

"Whatcha drinkin', Dave?" his gal asked me. Her head was buried in their fridge, that firm, big ass in black slacks wiggling as bottles clanked from deep within a drawer.

"We were there too, it's where I got this," he said, angling his head at me, making sure we saw the fleshy trench running from his jaw and up into his obnoxious haircut.

My girl squeezed my arm at the sight of it. "It's terrible, what you're all put through."

"Mom, can we come out now?" pled a small child from an unseen location. I sat up straight. My girl squeezed my arm even tighter. A beer bottle was in my face.

"Not yet," said her friend, handing me the beer. "Daddy's marine friends are still here," said Mom.

Furtively looking around the place, as a hand rubbed my leg, I noticed some big differences between the guy in the family portraits hanging on the wall and the lobotomy patient now asking me what unit I was in. It all made sense, the whole thing. A hand crept northward up my thigh.

Our hostess, as per standard operating procedure, had stowed her sons in a room, maybe a broom closet, while "Daddy's marine friends" were over.

"Her husband is deployed," my girl whispered in my ear. I shook my head absently, trying to fight off the likely facial expression of an extremely insulted intelligence. "Does that bother you?" she asked.

"None of my business, I guess."

Here I met an undefined moral conflict, however, made all the thicker as I realized how all people involved were somehow connected by the Culture of the Deployed.

Before long we all made off to our awaiting beds. The fair-skinned, infidelity-prone homeowner guided her life-support system for cock to the master bedroom. My girl and I, however, were given one of the imprisoned children's bedrooms. There are likely many who would concede that there's something thrilling about throwing a stuffed animal off a bed to lay down an excited lover.

Next; no condom, no pretense, no tomorrow.

In the morning I awoke to rays of sunlight, peering out from between Spiderman blinds. Olive skin atop skin of ink and white, she smelled the way the wild orange groves did back in Florida—the ones I had found hidden in Wekiwa, after a faint rain and the sun had come through the patches of cypress canopy. Although I had a Lego digging into my hip, the moment of closeness was not lost. She awoke and smiled with the half of her face not pressed against my chest.

"Good morning, animal," she said. Indeed. I climbed on top of her. She seized mine with her own, endearingly.

The bedroom door creaked as it opened, and her face reacted in horror as her womanhood corresponded in a rapid demoistening. Then the shriek of a mortified boy emitted up my back, crawling up like a damn spider.

"Get out!" yelled out from underneath me. I tried to make my ass somehow disappear. The door shut. Any thought of my assistance in traumatizing a military brat any worse than he already was was squeezed out of me by tan legs and tossed out of the room with a kiss.

Avoiding a military brat of my own, at the last second, where my face looks like I'm having a stroke and I speak in some dead language, I pulled out and came on the Charlie Brown sheets.

The breakfast after was as odd as one would imagine it to be. The boys were officially let out of the room. POWs[66] seeing the sun for the first time in what could have been days, they walked cautiously, like dogs detecting a problematic scent.

---

66   Prisoner of war

Chastised thoroughly for not being able to find one of my socks, I was finally able to get into my truck and get the hell out of there.

There were a few more rendezvous, all progressively going the same direction—downhill. Come to find out, being even remotely a part of her daily life came with a swarm of annoyance. Reigning supreme was her pit bull, a spoiled creature that rivaled a Saudi prince who'd demanded to sleep in her bed and would whimper and howl if locked out. I once waited for her to go take a piss. Grabbing the controller for the dog's electric collar, I proceeded to juice that rodent until her bathroom door cracked opened. I met her ten-year-old son, too. This meeting was actually a sigh of relief. It confirmed her story that she was separated, rather than pulling any antics learned from her friend. Be that as it may, her kid was as pleased with my presence as he would've been if locked out of his room with his sheets jizzed on.

The final meeting was sexless and brief. Her son's dad had filed something, apparently hurting her purse in the process. "I fucking hate men!" was the last thing I heard as I egressed from her tantrum. Once back in the barracks, I logged on; there were messages in the inbox.

16

CLEAN AND GREEN VS. THE GOTH

WINTER 2003

ONE RANDOM ORLANDO NIGHT while on leave, myself, my dad, and a good civilian friend of mine all went to a local pool hall. Owned by a friend of my dad's, I had played in the vacant lot behind the bar as a kid, cautiously pilfering through the encampments of the homeless and chasing around a flock of peacocks that had congregated there for as long as anyone could remember. This was the kind of place that Quentin Tarantino would salivate over when scouting for shoot locations. Placed in the deep shadows of a thicket of oak, it sat happily on the border of where two trailer parks met with the farthest shores of a little southern ghetto.

To enter the bar, before walking through the first set of double doors, one would pass a hedge row. Here a group of men, years later, would hide out to mug drunk patrons. I recall the one night when my friend and I encountered this group. They came out of the shadows the same way moccasins come out of their nests—quickly, but only a short distance. They assessed my friend and me. At the time I'd just gotten out of the military and was roofing houses. There is something about "I work fifty hours a week running terra-cotta tile up a ladder with guys who have *110% Peckerwood* inked on their backs" that apparently screams "fuck with the next guy." My buddy was no slouch either, though slimmer than me and void of much of the underworld dealings that I had accrued. He and I had just finished reading the Black Medicine series and were anxious to try some tricks out on someone.

A few nights prior, after all the bars had closed, we found a man sleeping in his truck outside a day labor office. Figuring it a great chance to practice some jiu jitsu and maybe even some takedown defense, we asked him politely to exit his vehicle. After much coaxing, we convinced him we just wanted to borrow a lighter. His intuitions correct, the moment his back was turned I drunkenly went in for the takedown. Perceiving a savage robbery, his fight-or-flight kicked in with enough adrenaline to slip out of my hold and run madly into the street. He immediately flagged down a passing cop, resulting in our most frantic egress.

Anyway, these muggers, possessing those innate analytical skills that human predators often do, retreated back to their bushes and shadows. About twenty minutes later, after my cohort and I had worked ourselves into a good game of pool, a group of three came bursting in, blood spewing from one of their heads, claiming they had been beaten and robbed.

I recall the taste of satisfaction and pride; years of the hard road had etched themselves onto skin and demeanor, and those muggers had seen it. I was all the more tickled that the victims looked like the soft white kids that spent a month's pay at FUBU, all to be decimated by the very street archetype they so desperately tried to emulate.

So, passing the hedges, passing a first set of double doors, traversing a tiny room, and then a second and final set of doors, patrons find themselves in something like a larger version of Moe's tavern off *The Simpsons*. Shit like Patsy Cline and Jim Croce playing, while rehabilitated hookers turned pizza-joint managers sit next to the disheveled forgotten, crawling out of society's bilge to occasionally suck down a few cold ones.

On the night in high remembrance, we all walked in and to my delight, I heard some heavy metal playing. Directly in front of me was the back of some colossal beast dressed in black, with hair of equal pitch ending below the shoulders. The bar itself had multiple fronts, and at the one closest to the doors, he was the only person occupying an entire bar-face. People weren't displaying any outright fear per se, but the wide berth given to him as he banged his head and pounded the bar was instantly noticeable. He wasn't terrifying by any means, the way say a junkyard dog is; rather he was that dog with beady eyes that made everyone guess if he had rabies or not. Although mostly looking straight down at his crossed forearms resting on the bar, he soaked in all the attention from the cautious can collectors and check cashers scurrying about his periphery.

We posted up at a corner pool table.

"If there are any Christians in here, you better cover your fucking ears!" The big Goth had made his way to the jukebox.

We were in need of some drinks. I was basically there to watch. My buddy and my dad were both amazing pool players. The most entertaining aspect about it, however, was that while my buddy got consistently worse the more he drank, my dad got consistently better. At a few pitchers in, some sort of competitive equilibrium was established and it became a worthy spectator's sport.

Naturally then, it was my job to get the beer when it was needed. There was a clear open space at the bar. More than that, though, there was a clear opportunity to test fate. I figured, what the hell, and perched right next to the Goth who was back on his stool headbanging and pounding the bar with his fists. Upon closer inspection, he looked to be Puerto Rican, hair shining due to the sweat, over six feet tall, about 250 pounds, and sporting (among other things) a USMC tattoo on his arm. It was one of those classic barroom moments, right out of a western—the slow, upwardly rotating glare from his glass to my face.

I rarely found clothing or anything traditionally regarded as "style" that I really liked, or fit me well. For whatever reason, the Marine Corps undershirt, coming in olive drab, known commonly as the skivvy shirt, fit me like a glove, and I would proudly wear it whenever and wherever. It always made me feel like Henry Rollins in his video for "Liar" for some reason. Originally seeing the video in seventh grade on a *Beavis and Butt-Head* episode, I was struck profoundly by the synthesis he emitted: military, punk, tough nerd, and animal. I guess I fancied myself all those things too, and I always liked flying a barroom door open sporting the OD[67] green. This night was no exception.

The Latino, gothic, one-man show growled at me, "You in the Corps?"

The challenge was something palpable—thick enough, in the space between us, to register on a high school chemistry weight scale. Like two mountain goats or tomcats outside your window at 4:00 a.m., or some species of aggressive seal, a confrontation seemed imminent.

One of the more interesting things about marine culture is the complex web of who deserves an ass beating, and when. In the same day, hell, the same bar, a group of boots can get their asses kicked by some seasoned POGs for wearing too much USMC propaganda out in town. Some other boots kick a civilian's ass for not knowing the difference between Operation Iraqi Freedom and Operation Enduring Freedom. Grunts then stomp a POG for wearing the wrong shirt, and then finally the POGs, boots,

---

67   Olive drab

and grunts join forces to beat the dog shit out of the civilian reinforcements that arrived to avenge their friend's ass beating an hour prior.

With this in mind, the meeting of two marines in a seedy bar is not necessarily one of certain merriment and brotherhood. Civilians tend to get tripped out by this, and all I can offer for an explanation is a fierce proprietary nature.

"Yeah man, stationed in Lejeune, home on a ninety-six," I said. "Right on…brotha."

The bartender brought me my pitchers, looking at the other guy out of the corner of his eye. I left with a nod and returned to our corner. While away, my dad apparently had to take a piss and had disappeared in the cigarette smoke at the far side of the bar.

Maybe one Slayer song later, the abrupt squeaking of barstool legs rubbing against the tile floor hit my ears. A hammer fist against the bar and then the yell of "All right, Marine! Front and fuckin' center."

I had no idea what compelled me exactly, but I found myself marching like a zealot to the stake. It was on. Stupid violence. The thought of the battle was exhilarating. "St. Vitus' Dance" by Sabbath was at its halfway point. Gloomy, powerful riffs wrapped themselves around my arms and legs. I didn't know what to expect, other than a glorious and vicious scrapping it out of two generations of bar-fight aficionados. He had slid the stool back, walked a few feet toward me…and then stopped. Just the moment prior to planning that first punch, the one you hope goes right down a motherfucker's throat and sets you up for the glorious sit-on-chest-and-punch-face-until-tired, just before that moment I saw the shots he had set up on the bar.

His scowl had turned into goofy grin. I was taken aback by the childlike way his cheeks fattened and his toothbrush commercial smile emerged from his outlaw beard.

Unfortunately for him, my dad, who had apparently also heard his perceived challenge from across the bar, had procured a girthy pool stick and was steadily making his way toward the guy's back. He had confidence in his son, sure. But a little assist wouldn't hurt. With stick in hand, like a ninja wielding a katana, my dad had his eyes set right on the back of the guy's head, which on the other side, unbeknownst to my father, displayed the face of an Italian merchant, gracious at the sight of his first customer of the morning.

Forced to morph instantly from "combat mode" to "preventing my dad's certain death mode," I smiled, laughed, and grabbed a shot glass.

CEASE FIRE!

What transpired was a night of banter that ended up in a bear hug and lamentably a few "oorahs" from my new friend.

Months later I found out that my parents went back to that same bar, met him again, ended up giving him a ride home, and he cried on my mom's shoulders about God knows what, asking her if he could call her Mom.

17

EMAILS FROM THE AL ANBAR

As the son of the willfully technologically regressed, I'd never used email prior to deploying, possibly setting me apart from the millennial brood more than any other attribute. While tackling the quandary of logging on, saving contacts to a newly discovered address book, and replying, I emailed multiple people back in the USA about multiple things. Due to operational tempo, emailing was a sporadic event. Below, as a select sample, are three emails per month of my OIF IIB deployment. The recipient(s) have intentionally been left anonymous. Looking back through these, I'm tickled by their youthful nature, the telling infatuation with books and music, and left proud of who I was. Yet it's impossible not to acknowledge a shadow that exists atop a portion of these messages. Being deeply insecure while highly motivated made for an interesting early twenties.

These emails are in almost pure original form, edited minimally only when grievous grammatical errors occurred, likely due to being rushed out of the Internet centers and/or prediscovery of spell-check.

9/17/04

Just read your emails along with Chris' and Kim's. I'll write kim back later when I have more time. i'm writing you for the purpose of giving yall some levity due to the fact that Fallujah is getting some intense media attention. i'm sorry but we are directly ordered not to tell anyone anything about what's going on here that the cameras don't or won't film, so you won't hear much from me again. I'd rather keep you informed, I think it is a more comforting tool than lies or silence, but it's for our own operational security and I agree with it. I don't have anything to tell you except I'm here and I'm going to be here for awhile. Take care and I'll write again pretty soon.

9/25/04

That's interesting about Greg's birthday bash, you'll have to keep me informed. I haven't been able to go to the gym in 5 days, I know that sounds like a funny complaint being in a combat zone but never the less it's here and I want to use and abuse it. We've been busy and the tempo is getting exciting. 2 years of baseball practice and I'm on the diamond. I'm always adjusting shit and trying to better myself but I'm almost always left with the humbling, but smile-producing fact that alot of these guys are better than me at most of this, my times up and I gotta go.

9/26/04

We kicked ass today, found over 100 lbs. of explosives and ran over 300 cars through check point. I'm pretty tired but I'm going to the gym after this. It's 8:56 pm here and I've been up since 8 am yesterday. We did good and some big wigs were impressed with the platoon. You need to brace yourself, if the power still on the tv is going to be spitting out some intense shit. I don't mind that yall pray for me but I don't really care either. This stuff has become so job-like and programmed that we think too rational to sympathize with praying loved ones an ocean away. I emailed laura and kim, I tried chris, but his address is weird. I just recently fell in love with the song by neil young, that starts off "my, my, Hay, Hay," and says "rock n roll will never die" a lot. I bet kim or jake know the song. I don't know if I told you this but oct. 1, dana and kate each receive their dozen flowers along with my address.

I'm not saying this to dramatize or sound all out there or even make you more aware, I just think you need to know that something's at a boiling point but instead of being weak and insecure chose to be confident in the situation, god knows I am.

10/03/04

This is the first day where I didn't want to be here, temporarily, me and my team leader really got into it, in each others' face and cussing a storm. It's due to a lot of inner team conflict that isn't worth writing about.

Anyways I got promoted the other day. CORPORAL, 1 under Sergeant.

As I think of it i need u to send me some stuff (I got your package of towelettes and food by the way): I need for you to go to GNC and get me CE2, Ripped fuel and send me the remainder of my N02 I had in my truck.

I don't like dealing with the Iraqi people, I'm not a cop and I don't speak Arabic, mighty unqualified if u ask me. I don't have any sympathy on them either, you can't trust any of them. The shriek of the kids when they see the males being taken away blindfolded was eerie at first but is now pretty comical. none of that jaded Viet vet Hollywood BS but you get used to dealing with them as inferiors very easy. My side note, now that mom has power of attorney I want her to put the $ in my union account into my saving with Marine Federal. Also if you can check and see under my checking account if the transaction of the flowers to the girls was ever cleared.

I've been thinking about tina turning 16 this month and how time has split us into two different echelons of life and of thought. I know her less than anyone in the family, the corps and the road has insisted I miss a lot of things, and I don't always realize it right away.

P.S. mom conservative with the emails ok and if you guys don't get one from me for a couple of weeks don't bugg out!

10/27/08

I never have enough time to unload all I want to say to you gotta take this rough draft as final. I got you and nanny's letters today. you both have distinct handwriting. Me and tina's is horrible and I can't figure out where it comes from. I guess I want to tell you that I sometimes feel bad that we never see each other anymore. Mom has told me how my being away has made your life a little duller and less testosterone induced. I know you realize that I had to go and I'm going to stay out there for a long time. I can't sit still (even being mortared can be boring). I can't stomach where we grew up and I never ever get homesick. I think the symbol of future success is a middle finger to a hometown! Regardless it hits me like clock work anytime I listen to CCR, or lately van Morrison, I miss something. Maybe that's why ambition and discontent put you up to a harsh light where I can say now that I was too hard on you. For some reason I randomly picture a baseball being thrown really high up on dann st., or you and bob smokin' grass on a beach, or you running on the golf course as a kid w/ the song "mrs. Robinson" playing. I really don't know why but it fills me with emotion.

I gotta go

10/30/04

I can see those pics without assistance thank you. Anyway, that one you saw was when the other guys were changing over all their ammo to us. That was a 250 rd. belt of 50 cal. Ammo that is in our vehicle as we speak. The guy on the left is our gunner in our team. the guy in the background is Dez, the assistant team leader and a sniper in the platoon. Dad met him.

I think you and everyone else need to quit praying for our fucking safety! The hand of God can really make life boring (knock on wood). If anything, pray that our command grows a pair of nuts and lets us get some, we work under cowards and politicians. If God wants to save me from death and injury, then good, but please don't let it be by riding the bench! (a breath later) as you can see it's starting to get boring and the operators are getting restless.

11/01/04

We don't wear that goofy shit on our helmets!

11/22/04

I wouldn't mind, but don't mention a fucking word about me.

11/26/04

Well whatever yall did I got a message from Dana. They got 'em. Katie threw a fit like I figured she would so Dana said she didn't want to write me out of respect for her. I understand. Dana's mom told Katie to get over it and Dana to write!

Thanksgiving was less than a joy to say the least!

Also EVERCLEAR (the cd that has the song "father of mine" or "daddy gave me a name".

Bye bye

12/02/04

Tuna was definitely eager to get back. He said Bagdad is full of people in their own world, like there's no war going on.

Another is gone and this time a toddler is left fatherless. The guy was as trained as one of us could ever get, over a decade in service. fragile is the word of the day.

I'm not surprised on how unaffected I feel, maybe I'll realize it later.

Guess what? I ran into my fucking recruiter in the chow hall. We chatted but I did bring up as professional as possible that he screwed me. I think he remembered everything! He says he's been here since april!

Seeya

12/04/04

I emailed steve stewart twice. Did he get em. That's surprising john looked real good. I figured he was on a downward spiral.

My contract is fine now. it's just all the time I spent in ft. sill and arty, I could have been going to real recon schools and training packages. Time ill spent for the most part!

That's good tina isn't a bum. Hopefully she doesn't get too stressed out.

12/13/04

Ya, I don't want a damn thing from anybody!

Also, our opsec has tightened so no more clues and drunken rants. People have given out info that got back to the wrong people.

I'd like that simon and garfunkel cd, though!

01/26/05

I've been emailing henry rolling back and forth for 2 days now! My life has some meaning!

More stuff:

Rollins band "end of silence"

Black crowes "shake your money maker" Spin doctors "pocket full of kryptomine" I know it's some $$, thanx a bunch.

01/28/05

Yall really messed up by giving my email to Lew Scruggs. I get 3 dumb ass letters a day. It's ok though.

Books (don't send)

Conrad's "In the Heart of darkness"

f. scott fitzgerald "the great gatsby" evan wright "generation kill" bill me later!

Rollins and I talked about the BS in Iraq & I told him how many fans he has in RECON.

01/31/05

Well the elections are over, we had a small hand in security. A few moments of violence and a lot of talking to the people. I'm on a mission to learn all the animal names and teach them the English equivalent. Chelub=dog, ezmalay=donkey

Nothing else to say really.

02/02/05

I remembered an early memory the other day.

I remember in preschool dad coming and picking me up and taking me to the fair.

He had on those dark blue work pants and that maroon wind breaker that he still has.

It's so weird how this place makes you think.

I've been really happy lately. We have been operating out of an ammo supply point run by civilian contractor. No BS marine corps, like wimps who never leave the gates telling us what it is to be a good marine. I've been working out harder than I ever have in my life. Me & tuna are putting up some heavy weight, and I've taken the bull by the horns as far as the minor leadership roles a corporal is in duty to. there is a guy here that looks just like dad. Maybe that's why all these off memories and things are surfacing.

02/15/05

Does the battalion email you with dates on our return? I hear april 10th. I should be in lejeune, but don't know 100%.

Ya time is flying. I feel like I'm going on 45. I can say that I truly grew up in recon. The tugs, painting, mosh pits, boot camp, first

1.5 years in the corps, I was still something that I'm not anymore. I,m planning on emailing you a sample of the writing I have been doing over here. It's almost always, short dark, and gives the vibe of a drunk folk singer on a poorly lit stage.

02/17/05

Please please print this or something (only way I can figure out how to contact jake)

Jake,

Music truly branded itself in and on me. I listen to DOWN in the gym, and when I heard "cemetery gates" the other day I just stood there thinking. I miss ya, and I can't wait to see ya at the river soon & I can't wait to introduce you to a few of my wartime buddies.

I figured out OUR tatt's. I'm gonna get the CFH brand on my opposite shoulder of the get some go again piece & you get those on your wrists!! What do you think. I'll finance this endeavor and I think it would be awesome.

Keep up the fight for your boy. He deserves more. Happy late birthday dude!

03/02/05

I wasn't saying in the least that turning 22 in the heat of a greenside hide with 2 of my best friends with enough power to wipe out eagle blvd was a "crappy birthday". I was practically bragging!

I can get drunk and shit on any day. I wouldn't trade this one for much.

Last year I turned 21 at ARS on a Monday morning log run where we came in dead last!! Ha! Look at it, a year for recon!

03/23/05

I've been busy tanning and working out these days. The new recon boys are here and we are data dumping our deployment on them to set them up for success. I have to go out for 2 days starting tomorrow night and I'm done with combat operations.

I gotta tell ya, this place has changed. The marines from the east coast have taken over and the original fighters have retrograded back to the states or are planted. This place is hardly a war zone anymore and these new people's attitudes are pissing me off!

There is so much involved with "war" that will piss off a set of open eyes and ears that it is best just to walk away from it (i.e. people who never left the gate bragging to girls about how many people they killed. It is so childish. I just tell myself" they know deep down who did what").

03/31/05

What's up with the pics?

Tina told me she has lost almost ten pounds. Is that from exercise or being sick?

I saved the flight times in a folder but make sure you hold on to them, too!

Oh, I got and consumed the last package. Chase got destroyed and pissed all over another guy's clothes!!

04/03/05

I am leaving camp today so chances are I won't be able to contact you via phone or computer for the rest of the deployment.

04/03/05

We had a small fuck up, so I am here one more night.

04/06/05

I leave for Kuwait tonight. Tq is the camp I am at right now. Its an air field.

18

GAVE YOU EVERYTHING

FALL 2007

REGARDING POTENT WORDS AND phrases, literal meaning has been practically raped right out of the English language. "I'm starving," says the morbidly obese person at the fudge fountain, "go to hell" from the scorned teen, "I'm too exhausted to move" from the hung-over bartender or mid-management *yes man* at the cluttered desk. Strange thing to get tripped up about? Maybe. But language painted with such broad brush strokes both dulls critical faculties and smacks of a culture of leap-before-they-looks who sacrifice aesthetics on the altar of melodrama.

"Gave everything." This phrase may also be worthy of being lumped onto the heap of the worn-ragged. It sticks in my head because it is but one of many banner slogans that were squeezed dry during the emergence of the warrior-themed sports. For me at least, an honest assessment indicates a giving of everything twice in my life. Well, one more an era, the other a specific day. ARS and a fight: I felt the most beautiful of pains.

In 2007, I was fresh out of the Corps, still highly energetic, but unfortunately realizing for the second time why exactly I had joined in the first place.

It must be understood that in the heart of many warriors drums the occasional beat of pure misanthropy. While this sinister little thump varies from trigger-puller to trigger-puller, there's no doubt a disgust for pallid social norms exists prior to donning the uniform. For most it grows wildly before it withers, if it withers at all.

Orlando: truly in many ways a failure in social engineering. It's a plethora of mediocrity, cheap land molested by anything ready to uproot what little culture the place had and exchange it with an asphalt parking lot and mall music. For the few actually born there, there lingers this Jeffersonian aggregate farming ideology, resulting in having children at socioeconomically inopportune young ages as if it were some badge of honor.

These societal uglies thrived untouched while across an ocean transpired the eighteen-round fire-for-effect (FFE) against Baghdad, the countless small arms engagements, and all the IEDs in the Triangle of Death. Coming back home to America, not much changed for many lower-middle-class kids who weren't ready for college yet, or much anything else, really.

The Disney Waste Land! Look at its thoroughfares, such a lie. Come experience the Magic, yes, but please stay awhile and experience our felonious extravaganza, our prolific drug epidemic, our terrible traffic, and the fatal attitudes that come with it. Come experience our hilarious education, religiosity. Come enjoy the subdivisions that emerge like mushrooms, in a matter of months occupied by confused transplants, smelling of some unnameable failure from their home states. Come enjoy the land where having no culture becomes the culture of the land. Where a bright billboard for some "family-oriented" attraction, built by a divorced man with an oxycodone addiction who's the father of a teenage, latch-key son, blinks blindingly at you from I-4. The shadows created by such hide the scurrying of the lost, medicated creatures who stalk the lower areas where God and Mickey are almost certainly not to be found.

Suffering the rain and the scorching sun stands the two-story world. Low buildings, probably all built by the same contractor and in the same year. A fucking mile of nothing but fast-food restaurants, their clever billboards trying to outdo the business to their left or to their right. The low humming sadness, hanging just above the power lines.

I found myself back in this ogre and before long began to panic from the claustrophobia.

A gym, now closed, used to pump and growl near the slow but unstoppable growth of a religion-owned health care juggernaut. Advertised as the oldest gym in Florida, this hole-in-the-wall was something out of *Rocky*. No AC, no machines, and no yoga pants. Bouncers and bikers and felons and cops and professional wrestlers congregated in this iron shrine. Feats like "incline press-535" recorded on the wall, while a guy fresh out of prison with an 82nd Airborne tattoo preacher curls 135.

I had started to go to this gym while still on active duty. When home on leave, I'd make my way in there whenever I could. The new owner, whom is most aptly described as what a homeless man would look like if injected with ten gallons of HGH and two quarts of diesel, allowed me to train for free. This gruff owner, rumored to have gone to Japan to fight some robot prior to official ownership, felt it his patriotic duty to allow all 165 life-takin', heart-breakin' pounds of my flesh to train itself into a vascular fortress. It was through him I met an ex-con, out on an attempted murder charge, who got me into MMA before the world knew the word *affliction*.

I had kickboxed as a kid; however, my pugilistic days never developed—well, not in any formal way. So it was a pleasant return to both physical discipline and purpose when I started going to the ex-con's countertop warehouse to train in some basic MMA.

He trained elsewhere as well, but he agreed to teach me the basics of Brazilian jiu jitsu and the *lost art of hooking*—catch wrestling.

For several weeks I trained and sparred with him and his band of merry men, a group of heavily tattooed construction types, usually with southern accents.

All was well until the day the SWAT team raided the place.

I wasn't there, but found out later the location was some sort of drugs and/or weapons cache for some white supremacist group. I never got the full story, and that is likely because the day after it occurred, I blindly walked into the aftermath and the remaining guys gave me an interrogation. Some were less convinced than others, but it was an interesting feeling to hear the type of charges, look around, and see at least a few faces thinking they found the rat.

Martial arts were to be put on hiatus for a while, and I was told to look into an official MMA gym on the other side of town. I was there the next day.

From the moment I stepped inside until the moment I stopped competing about a year later encapsulates a very alive ribbon in time. I was able to meet and even spar with people whom I'd watched win and lose in the UFC. Several months in, I decided to shed the ground game though, fall back on childhood skills, push the forte, and compete as a kickboxer.

Put on an amateur Muay Thai team, I traveled Florida for six months and got to experience the thrill of a first-round knockout, the humbling experience of losing in front of my friends, and the desperate exhaustion when neither you nor the other guy has been beaten bad enough to fold, and the bell refuses to ring.

By the time I put in my mouth guard for my final match, I had switched gyms three times and coaches twice. Twenty-five pounds lighter than when I had started this new warrior road, I'd just accepted a position as a police officer for a city that strikingly resembled the dip-spittin', monster truck gettin' stuck, GED maybe, denim nightmare that was the fight card's host: Lake City.

My third and final Muay Thai match, my entire team came to fight an opponent. We drove from Orlando, ending our road trip at the entrance of an industrial Quonset hut. It was massive and cheap and for four-wheeled machinery to be stored during rains, repair, or anticipated biblical plague.

For whatever reason, I was slotted second to last on the fight card. The last fight, the main event, was rightfully so. The guys were machines...and I was going on right before them. Had I been recognized as the link between a main event fighter and the undercard? I could ponder that later. Someone in the distance kicked a heavy bag—*thuwack*! I had more pressing matters at hand.

Weighing in at a sickly 151 pounds, I scanned and inventoried the growing crowd. The slow southern drawls all came together in unison to chant for their hometown hero. He was as tattooed as me, but where I earned mine on docks and in squad bays, his were more after flipping the Ford, a keg party, or celebration after stomping some rival group of perfectly equal people.

And that was the gist of it, come to find out. Two or three gyms came to the throw down. While some competed against other school-trained fighters, the horde of local rednecks, who came to test their wind and beat some ass, took up about half the fight card.

My opponent was school-trained: a young black guy with an eight-pack, polite and quiet, who had shaken my hand earlier and then sat in a corner to wrap his own.

What a scene in the back staging area. Fighters prepped; stretching, jump roping, praying. The redneck opposition;

standing around, smoking cigarettes, watching us, somewhat surprisingly in admiration.

It began. A bell rang, and a sparsely packed metal hut roared.

Fights started. Fights ended. A man came back to the staging area pouring small rivers of sweat, and another man took a breath then walked out into the arena. My team was going through the night undefeated. An additional pressure to any new competitor who's completely honest with themselves.

It was my time to enter the ring.

Now this may sound as guilty of melodrama as any "I'm starving" comments, and from a professional fighter that criticism is certainly understandable, but—when the ring floor has been wiped clear of the last fight's residue and the crowd starts stirring, looking toward the entrance to see who is going on next, your stomach drops. There is no way out of the situation, and there is a piece of you that oh-so wants there to be. Next, a wave of emotions and physiology pummels you up and over: not wanting to let your coach down, yes; complete tunnel vision, that too; and a pure desire to put the other guy to sleep.

The first Thai fight, I knocked my opponent out so quick I barely broke a sweat.

The second one, I was beaten like a redheaded stepchild for three agonizing rounds.

I left my gym due to that fight. Losses come, but my blurry-eyed coach seemed a bit more interested in a ring girl than his fighters.

My new coach, now in my corner, had put a lot into my training and I felt an obligation I couldn't explain. My polite, long-armed, eight-packed opponent entered his own corner. His face set with his jaw poked out, his eyes shiny white bullets. I think prayer is a silly thing in most circumstances, but I did say right then something to the effect of "let my labor show."

The bell rang. He tucked his jaw in. I made my way to him. He met me in the middle.

Equal in size, virtually equal in training and ability, he and I beat the ever-loving piss out of each other. In the first round I backed him into his own corner and had him wobbling. I saw those bullet eyes roll into the back of his head, but it just wasn't enough. Soon he began to rely on the Thai clench, and at one point got me down with a trip. My oh my, how the drunken crowd howled at a good exchange, and, my oh my, how they booed during a lock-up that lasted more than half a second. He was immensely strong. My wind started to give, and the yells from both corners could have been from the North and South Pole. Any sense of time had gotten KO'd in the first round. Everyone and everything seemed a million miles away, except the blue, sweating ring under your feet and your opponent experiencing the same harsh reality you are. Simultaneously punching the other, both backing up, wobbling, then colliding again...it raged on. It was like being in the belly of some huge animal. Quonset hut ribs and overhead lighting, mixed with the smell of hay and cheap beer.

In the end it was a draw, leaving my official amateur fight record at 1-1-1(1). It always makes me laugh, considering my existentialist proclivities.

I gave all I had in that fight—*gaaaave everything, man!*—as paltry as the setting and results may seem to some. I know this because in the street fights I got into as a kid and the few barroom brawls as an adult, I always cared about getting hit. The concern waxed and waned, but it was ever-present in the chaotic actions and reactions. Not this fight. Toward the end of this match, any technical skill I had gave way to desperate and winded haymakers.

He did the same. I had to be helped out of the ring and was placed at an empty table, where I sweat and bled. A few guys came up to me at some point: "That was a fuckin' war, bro!" Indeed.

I hadn't felt that pure pouring-out sensation since my ARS days.

Those who have been there know when what's deemed safe and sane takes the backseat to some wild desire. Pushing through physical and mental torture, sidestepping the blood clots and somber nights, goals are gripped—frivolous to many who don't like the sight of their own blood, short-lived for most who do—highlights of many lives who found happiness out in the margins.

19

HEDONISM IN DUBAI

FALL 2010

THE CABIN WAS A flying Pringles can. It was stuffed with beards. It smelled like an armpit. From my window seat in the decrepit little plane I could see the Hindu Kush Mountains—fanning out their crooked spines in what was otherwise a sort of red-dust covered desert. The whole landscape looked so inhospitable, like a part of the world that had started to develop a billion years ago and had just given up somewhere in its early stages. Arabic murmurs lingered in my right ear as I followed the faint traces of rivers in the lowlands, draws and small plateaus resting between the Kush's fingers. Following the rivers had become a bit of a habit of mine, in transit. Sometimes, on the riverbeds, there were clusters of human inhabitance. The first time I saw these ancient circles and squares, they looked like what a satellite may pick up on Mars, or some other, distant planet if intelligent life were ever discovered. And that perception hadn't changed much, really, even after seeing them half a dozen times. The only additional thought, if any, was *how in the hell did they end up there in the first place?*

⟨⟨⟨⟩⟩⟩

MY TRIP WAS A series of conjoining yet very different flights.

First, the flight from Orlando to Atlanta. Boarding the flight from one's "home of record," the residue of your private life is still on you; it sticks to your clothes and in your hair. It's at this stage where the fellow passengers are the most normal, cut from the settler-fabric of the population. The family coming home from the Disney vacation, the college girl visiting her boyfriend, the techie bound for the big meeting—and then me, punched in the panorama like a bruise: the Asolo-booted, tattooed mercenary. All parties clean, bright-eyed, and with fully charged phones.

Once in Atlanta I would file out into the swarm. Past a food court and then maybe a frantically running businessman, I'd see the first sign that I was getting closer; a greying beard atop a North Face shirt. Drawing nearer my gate I'd see two more; tribal tattoos that vine down to the wrists, all coming out from under a shirt yelling "INFIDEL," talking to someone who looks like an African safari tour guide. Around an isle of ferns and a slight turn, and—there they are, at the mouth of my gate like bloodthirsty dogs, the motley crew of khaki-laden contractors.

These men were mostly out of ground combat jobs after one (extremely active) enlistment, a few were freshly retired after a full twenty, and all of them now putting their skills to use in the free market. They were earning five times more than when they'd held a rifle—in the exact same shithole—as a grunt, or as a Ranger, or as Marine Recon. It would soon be time again to guard important people, important places, and whatever else they paid us to. My spirit always lifted—always. A few head nods upon recognition, a smile, a handshake or two, and the solace that for the next couple of months I would be surrounded by men who viewed the world as I did, an ever decreasing occurrence as my years out of the Marine Corps stacked upon each other.

From Atlanta came the leviathan—the fifteen hour and forty-some-odd-minutes flight to Dubai. The amount of people that get on these flights is baffling; a couple hundred maybe. Who were these people? Where were they all going? Surely this cocktail of everything that is the West wasn't all destined to vacation on the Arabian Peninsula.

Boarding the double-aisle aircraft began the checklist. Acquire seat, check; music source and headphones, check; Ambien and hopefully a muscle relaxer, check; for some reason look around for the nearest hot chick and plan a way to fool around later, check; order a beer, check; as we fly up the east coast and angle towards Greenland—pass out in a hallucinogenic coma, check. This last check-in-the-box became increasingly necessary. The mind-numbing boredom of the transatlantic flight increased as the miles passed; scrolling through every video option available until I could recite their order and ratings in my sleep.

I wasn't alone in this feeling. One time, just prior to take off, a medic from my gig walked up and down the aisles, identifying his coworkers and handing out, to those of us in need, the proper dose.

"Hey, bro, you good?" he asked.

"Yeah man, hook me up, 'preciate it."

"No worries, I'm right behind ya—next to a family of fat asses, of course, if ya need any more. Hey, bro," he said, eyeing a comrade and heading toward the rear of the plane, "you good?"

The other white people, inexplicably in route to the Middle East, watched in tight-lipped curiosity as one burly arm after the other reached out to take a pill from the mysterious man of seat 37F.

Wheels up. Pills eaten.

The person in the middle seat would rustle against my arm, pulling me out of the drug-induced haze. Harsh slivers of light would shine through cracked window shades, a sudden bump of the wheels on the tarmac, and we were in Dubai. The great East-meets-West. The city where a Muslim man in a starched dishdasha will fly past you in a red Lamborghini, where kissing your wife in public can get you in a legal shit storm—while cheetah-printed flocks of Russian hookers wait in every worthwhile hotel lobby. Marching out of the giant plane, usually something like "Sweet Leaf" by Sabbath coming from my headphones, the sudden blast of wind from the Persian Gulf, and its eternal lover—the heat—awakens even the groggiest dullard, "You are now in a different world, motherfucker."

It's perhaps important to know that the contract life operates on a strict on/off ratio. On meaning "on project," off meaning at home (or in Thailand or the Philippines as many expats choose, already half-erect and discussing antibiotics with their brethren as they board the plane). The ratios vary, some gigs 2 on/1 off, others 3 on/1 off or 1 on/1 off. I was on a 2 on/1 off set up.

After several of these rotations, one particular leg back to Kabul left myself and a couple dozen guys I worked with stranded overnight in Dubai.

Maybe it was the hangover from my frustrated life as a former recon marine; having done nothing short of dressing in drag as a police officer for the past several years. The charade was to transition from combatant to cop, and then act like I gave a damn. For far too long the charade twirled, then was suddenly over. Maybe it was me trying woefully to chase my active-duty high with friends who had all gotten out too—who knows? But the bomb was set to explode.

It all started in some courtyard, surrounded by bars. Reminded me of the types of beer gardens I'd see on the outskirts of Orlando. These were the places local cougars and MILFs would go out on the prowl after having sold Mother's china and the good towels to buy the newest twenty-something heartbreak-ware.

But this Dubai beer garden held no such gems.

What it did have was an entire UAE "biker gang." Biblical skin and the type of haircuts usually seen in full collaboration with sleek D&G shirts near Miami Beach: All this—the House of Abraham's skin and the South Beach Ferrari type—adorned in black leather cuts, sporting what appeared to be their club regalia. They were probably going to just let it go and fly about the highways all night. It made me wish I could be an honorary member, just for twenty-four hours. The embedded Westerner. The Infidel, certainly shunted to the back, but no bother. Wearing whatever cut I would be given, following the long, black iron snake of bikes as they ripped and roared down the same roads I had traveled by taxi only a few hours prior. Who would we be looking for, a rival gang? Maybe just try and avoid an Exuberantly Rich in his Enzo? Or—an extra-long strip of fresh blacktop, kicking it into gear and riding on the hot, night wind until dawn comes over the Gulf of Oman.

"Did Eric tell you he hooked up with some Irish girl here last time?" said Army Zakk, a title given to him due to his resemblance to a bald, 'roided up, Zakk Wylde.

"No fucking shit?" I said. "That little shit. Figures. That nice-guy routine." A copious amount of beer and a few mixed drinks were going down our collective gullet.

"Yeah, he said she just came up to his ass."

"You guys wanna just go ahead and grab our rooms now," said-asked a former marine grunt named Ron, "so we can get back out here?" Ron was a beast. His arms and tree-trunk legs had the rare honor of rivaling Zakk's. He was also levelheaded, a commodity valued like gold within tribal packs—especially in the unbridled vicinity of women and booze. The pack smelled his good idea. Tabs were paid while slamming the cups and bottles that remained. Before long, the hotel.

Standing in a massive, ornate hotel lobby, here, of course, the cool test began. The dumpy, peacetime-guy immediately looked down at his feet. I knew three who were definitely sticking together; Zakk, Ron, and a marine machine gunner who was some type of Mark Wahlberg/Dale Comstock synthesis. These three had gone through all the contract vetting together, worked on the same shift together, and whenever not working gym'd it together. I allied with them and was quickly given confirmation: I was in! We pulled in one more, Shawn, a lean, toe-shoed former army grunt from the 4th Infantry Division who was a tickling blend of hot and cold. While one of the most laconic and stoic on our contract, he was prone to crisp foul language that would come out of him like a pressure-release valve.

And that was the crew: five dudes dropping all our luggage off in a flamboyantly decorated presidential suite, and then quickly relinking with the other cells down in the lobby.

A sight prevalent in Dubai, and a few other hubs of the Islamic world, is clusters of contractors. At first glance they, we, looked so out of place. In many ways we were. Business was one thing, industries ranging from hospitality to fossil fuels resulted in a speckling of Westerners at all the main attractions. But we were in a different business. With few exceptions, we were practitioners in an industry that came with an up-close-and-personal look at the region; one that would never make it into a Department of State progress report.

All groups had been assigned their birthing, all passports had been confiscated at the front desk—we were ready to go.

As we walked off the final stoop of our hotel's entrance and made for some less-lit direction, a voice spoke out, "No cameras. Tonight doesn't exist." It was one of our shift leads. He then turned to me, "I'm coming with you guys," then before I or anyone else could say a word, "I already called for a few taxis." Without any clear objection, he attached himself to us; swelling us to six. As we clocked our way down an evening side walk, my eyes took in the group; an array of smiles, collared shirts, denim, and sinewy arms sporting various G-shock watches and Ranger memorial bracelets.

In most Muslim countries I'd expect an ear-splitting call to prayer to kick on right about then. Considering Dubai's wealth and rabid desire to seemingly outdo all feats of engineering, a death-star Mosque speaker was not out of the realm of prudent consideration. Fortunately for us, whether such a diamond of weapons-grade audio power existed or didn't, it seemed West had beaten back East, at least that night. There was nobody to step over, mid-prayer, and the business district was in a swarm.

The buildings, ranging from peach to shades of yellow, all maintained the sandy color of the world they stood on. About head-level, their neon signs burned, gold and red, "African Jewellery," "Al Waleed." Between the tall, lean walls were the alleys, and where all the action was. Foods, discounted jewelry, greeters for whorehouses, all working within their jurisdictions on the slabs of pavement that their fathers likely passed down to them, and whose grandfathers likely fought fist and tooth for. Vendors of Japanimation-quality pink and blue, some open, others with the aluminum door rolled down and locked.

Taxis arrived. Shuffling into my seat I was reminded that I'd been periodically sucking down pills and beer for the past day.

A cavernous growl came from my gut, my head vibrated furiously for just an instant and then I was back to normal. Tired? No, I wasn't tired. Drunk? Nah, a stage had been set. The chains had been greased and neutral had been kicked into first. Just where to now was all that really mattered.

Our shift lead, the self-appointed Number Six, I'd occasionally interacted with at work in Kabul. Not a bad guy by any means—kept a smile despite being in the crosshairs of close to half a dozen paternity suits—but he was the kind of guy that made you sigh when you saw him approach, knowing good and well it would be dinner before you finally got to leave for your lunch. He had contracted the low-ball gigs for years; everywhere from Bahrain to Kuwait, probably jawing ears off and stuffing himself into group taxis all the way. Now our reappointed leader and tour guide, he said with a bearish smile, "Boy do I got somethin' in store for you fuckos." In his hand he flashed a rubber like a cop badge.

I was a bit curious, admittedly, considering the crowd he planned on entertaining, not to mention this sexually schizophrenic city we were in.

We arrived at some bar. I drank until I jumped on Zakk like one of those god-awful AFN commercials—the bold paper-pusher coming home to his daughter, soon forsaking her toys to leap onto him via the made-for-television flying squirrel. Beer was spilled, an English woman was soaked and appalled, and we were off to the next hard target.

Now rumor had been rumbling, long before this convoy, of a famous whorehouse, nay—whore compound. So when we pulled up to a bustling three-story building—men in khakis filing in and women in skirts and high heels leading them—the "somethin' in store for us" lost all its mystery.

"Whatta surprise," Shawn said. Indeed.

The few beers at the last place had skipped my guts and went straight for the veins. This meant the whorehouse-mecca's purple neon seemed Vegas-cool, but a moment later pulsated and banged. By the time the taxi doors closed, we were all getting pulled in.

Aiming for the honeycomb's center, techno music called to us as we passed through many thresholds; each one a step deeper, an abandonment of something while claiming something else—like Dante, or maybe Conrad. Through a dimly lit tunnel, and then— emergence, a...the...wide open belly. I recognized faces. *Holy shit man, it's the guys who didn't pass the cool test at the hotel*, I thought.

A nightclub more or less; the place was dark, except all the oranges, blues, and yellows that burst when the bass dropped. Standing at the mouth of this tunnel would've put a cop-turned-contractor into what we call "the black." All motor skills are useless and cognitive thought diminishes, leaving one basically a zombie—pure combat inefficiency. "Holy shit!" Ron shouted "This is a..." he pushed forward, shouldering for the main bar. I followed, hoping to utilize his draft.

Whores ran about the dance floor, swooping in on men like harpies. Beer splashed me, but it could have been sweat. I had to piss, but couldn't see a men's room door. Women hugged the perimeter, preventing even an inch of the wall from peering out at the dance floor. There were these sort of bleachers bolted against one, and perched upon them were hawk-eyed women. They had come from all over Africa, Lebanon, and God knows what other margins of developing countries and the almighty third world. Skin tones ranging from dark to a light mocha, all with hair adorned in their own best way to get at wallets. A man who'd shown me his CAC card at the Kabul embassy's front gate was now utterly surrounded. Woman fought over the men in languages I couldn't discern, drunk or sober.

A restroom had to be somewhere. I picked a cardinal direction, gritted my teeth, and mushed forward.

"Hi," someone said next to me. She—light skinned with wild curly hair—was now in front of me.

"Bathroom?" I replied.

She pointed the direction I was going, causing an inordinate amount of Hell Yeah in me for getting it right. I pushed past. She followed me.

Coming out, I didn't see her waiting, as I'd half-expected, and was soon reclaimed by the frantic sea of whores, making their mad dashes for anything that had a cock and a bank card. Fighting my way to the bar, exhausted and with a torn shirt, I order two beers. Panting, waiting, I look through a window. Far across the street a Mosque stood like a postcard from the UAE.

It was here that I had to make a command decision. The girls apparently had flapped away with everyone I had come with. Scanning the crowd, dodging the glares from the more aggressive hustlers, not one face was recognizable. Zakk, gone. Ron and the stoic Shawn, evaporated. Not even the CAC card guy could be found. While receptive to some action, yes, my need for it was abnormally subdued. This was probably due to the previous week spent in the Dominican Republic. The contractor abroad. Through the structure of my resort's liberated accommodations policy, I didn't have to leave my room, and wouldn't want nor need to. But, now—literally surrounded—the righteous dilemma every meat-eating, bear-killing man wishes to have actually arrived. *Do I just get stewed drunk and say fuck off ladies, or do a snag a few and get hammered later?*

I was alone, back against the bar, on an island in the fleshy sea of ill-repute. From over the bar, cast against the dancing lights and tops of heads, vague outlines of what appeared to be two men began to solidify. One short, one tall, I strained through the flotsam to discern faces of a couple guys who I worked with. Maybe they'd seen where everyone else had gone? Another beer slammed and a final one full and fresh in my grip, I began the icebreaker task of getting to them. Hands pawed at my arms, white teeth gnashed their business propositions, one I thought even went for my beer; but I kept pushing, pushing towards the small steps that would lead me up and out.

"Hi." Standing in front of me, blocking the staircase, her big eyes looking up at me in bright attentiveness. She had refound me. A glance up and I saw my two coworkers smirking at me. A glance back down and her face sensed my reluctance. She grabbed a passing coworker of her own. Standing next to one another, they were but a few shades off from being the exact same person. Belly shirt, perky breasts, dark pants. "Two?"

Sold.

Where was I to be taken? Would I find my friends there? Should I care? The three of us went out a side door of the club, hand in hand like a row of paper dolls. We entered one of the many waiting taxis and then took off down an alley. The nook snaked from cramped and silent to claustrophobic and seedy—and fast. My hope morphed from simply getting laid at a reasonable bargain to returning with my wallet and both of my kidneys.

"How far is this shit?" I asked, as I fought off a random upsurge of vomit.

"Not far, sir. You relax…" she said, as her friend caressed my arm. While it did come with a seductive little jingle, her voice also smacked with a sort of nudge that you're high in the running for being beaten and robbed. "Here we are," she said. There we were.

Stepping foot into the place, I was instantly back in Iraq: the cheap floors, the sparse furniture, the bags of rice piled in a corner, the random chords leading to various shoddy appliances such as box televisions.

Negotiations began. No shrewder reputation festers under the heavens greater than that of the Arab trader. I braced myself. To my surprise, however, their seeming enthusiasm made the first wad of Dirham the final price, as well as ridiculously propelling my drunken ego to almost uncharted heights. I was guided around a low, glass coffee table; I was laid, like an ancient king, on a thin bed that looked like a zebra-padded, sacrificial alter.

One switched on a nearby radio. Clothes came off as beer-coaster-size speakers kicked on. They put forth melodious chants and willowy background noises; like cats about to claw one another to death. The girls didn't utter a word, at least not to me, or in English, or anything I could ever remember.

In cases of very adventurous sex, the phenomenon of whiskey dick is interestingly absent. It's especially nonexistent when one woman is putting your condom on while the other is cradling your head in her lap, bare breasts swaying—all despite the general smell of burned rice and cheap, industrial cleaner.

Condom ready, one hopped on and the other crawled directly above my face. It began. Slightly spinning, and holding onto both of their left hips, I found myself in what was essentially the Kama Sutra meets the Abu Ghraib prison scandal.

Now I have heard tales of other *mercenaries*—without god or master—going down on hookers before. In some circles it's whispered to be a token of forsaking the world's normalcy. But wherever the truth lies, the noise of delight and astonishment that came from the superior end of our wobbling triangle left me inclined to believe it was a first occurrence in that bed.

Somewhere in the coital melee I ended up on top of both of them, the bottom one being crushed by a volley of pumps into the one above her.

"Sir, she no breathe—like this," squeaked the one getting it. It made sense, this reporting, she had a much better view of the other one's face.

"Sir—" then inaudible yells in language from their home countries.

"Cock yerr ass up," I said in rote, with an assist. I felt...it. Despite the contents swirling around in my gut and pumping in my veins, I felt it. Hot damn, and a Viking funeral for me!

That three seconds before you cum; that moment where you fight off the paralysis in your face, and you could live there forever. I struggled to stay a part of the twelve-limbed monster, to remain on the pile.

It was right then that I kicked my leg straight through the glass coffee table.

The freak-out of broken glass and blood climbed to a sudden and squealing height when one girl noticed the broken condom, wrapped around the base of my shaft like a messy ring toss. The orgasm-related vandalism and busted rubber were too much for them. Perceiving a dark figure in their midst, they backed up against the nearest wall and began to hiss and sneer like hyenas. Foot bleeding profusely, being wrestled to the ground by a stubborn pant leg, and hopping around the remains of her table—I frantically hobbled to the front door as objects flew past my head and shattered against the wall.

The taxi was still waiting out front. With my clothes twisted and wrapped, the torn shirt on backwards, and my right shoe beginning to make faint squishy noises, I dove in as the irate whores yelled their curses and witchery from their stoop. Pulling away, the driver, a man who looked exactly like the guy on the Izzy targets, remained expressionless as I burped out the long-forgotten name of my hotel.

Nauseous from almost two days of beer and sporadic, pill-fueled sleep, with the added ingredients of blood loss and hooker juice in my gums—I stuck my head out a rear window and puked my guts out.

Finally, upon reaching the hotel, my second wind had actually come back surprisingly well. Queasiness gone and wounds congealed, I limped past the huddle of western-dressed clerks, vigilant behind their marble, island counter.

I pressed my forehead against an elevator wall. My eyes shut as I listened to the *dings*, the elevator ascending floor after floor. A dribble of puke on my shirt, and what was surely a blood-soaked sock, a much-needed shower waited in the presidential suite. Exiting the elevator and approaching the suite's door, the raucous from the guys on the other side were things I should've been hearing. Nothing.

Something must have had happened. No one was there, but the aftermath of some great violence, or some flurry of pomp and raunch, was everywhere. The first thing that struck me was how a mattress had been lobbed against a wall. The large television on; nothing but fifty-two inches of analog TV snow.

Moans came from some undetermined location.

I was not alone.

Then more moans, but this time from the same room I was standing in.

Like Punxsutawney Phil maybe—from the thin space between the farthest bed and the wall, the smiling, bald-doofus head of Army Zakk popped up. "Sup, bro," he said.

Inching my way a bit closer, I saw he hadn't fallen off the bed. A naked Chinese woman, small breasts and skin like porcelain, lay pinned beneath him with her head on a rumpled pillow.

"What upppppppp?!" Behind me a door flew open. Tossing my head around to see, swaying in reinvigorated intoxication, out poured almost all of the original crew.

"Where is—"

"Yeah, he's still back there," the Marky Comstock machine gunner said, throwing a nod behind him. Ron was still ravaging the communal party favor in the adjoining room.

"What brand is that one?" I asked, smiling as I sat on the nearest bed and contemplated looking at my foot. But they didn't need to tell me. The shouts and yelps that soon came from that room were unmistakably Asian. A bizarre and trite skill to acquire perhaps, but it's that kind of subtlety that only certain types of men can detect, types often armed and outside the borders of most social norms.

Dominican a few weeks ago, North African and Middle Eastern earlier, *meh*—why not some Asian too? It was just a crotch-derived take on an Anthony Bourdain episode. Surmising the multicultural approach and tossed a condom, Zakk and I took his girl into the bathroom. A half-limp, wobbly H transpired. My ill fate with condoms struck again. Marky Comstock answered the call by opening the bathroom door and delivering some more rubbers in the multi-mirror flurry he once described to me as "tattoos and penis."

Second threesome of the night over, I had practically worked myself sober. Fueled and possessed by the lavish decadence that is

Dubai, bolstered by the presence of fellow neo-savages, I turned to our escort, just then opening the bathroom door. Wanting one last crack at it, as it were, I took her from the bathroom and into the third and final bedroom.

I don't know or recall in the slightest what happened next. If anything, the beer and blood loss got me. Upon coming to, she was squatting in the shower, washing herself. In the haze of the steam she looked like something from an old painting. I watched her, how she made feminine deliberate movements against the backdrop of ornate tile. I wondered how she got there, how long she would stay. There was something powerful and even otherworldly about her, despite her occupation; a type of honor during subservience that made a line out of *Devil's Guard* bounce around in my skull: "only capable of the Asian mind." And the feeling was not diminished, even as I threw her on the bed for one last go.

Girls gone, mattresses resituated, rubbers disposed of, showers executed—all relevant parties sat in their underwear around the table in our main room.

"Ok, room service said half an hour," I said, hanging up the phone.

"Cool. Fuck man, my fiancée can never know about this," Ron said. After a moment he continued, "Man, that little spinner could take it! I swore at any moment she was gonna yell *noo moe parachute, Dr. Jones.*"

Generals, chieftains, warlords going over their spoils.

"What happened to your fuckin' foot, man?" someone asked.

The television hummed a news channel speech about the merits of American foreign policy.

Room service arrived; colossal hamburgers, fries, and a final beer apiece. Standing in my boxers, wolfing down a clump of fries,

I couldn't help but relate how the night's events were strikingly similar to the barracks life, the golden age of brotherly insanity— just this time with a hefty paycheck and we were all over thirty, or damn close.

———

THE RIVER FORKED AS we continued east. Soon it split in two, making an island littered with clusters of Afghan huts.

Consecutive days of flagrant decadence are a vampire, and I was thoroughly drained. I sat still, somber; the bandages around my foot impeding my last remaining drops of energy from puddling on the dirty aircraft floor. The usual bevy of concerns lurked up; what blood tests were now necessary, and what horrors they may find. My eyes strained to pick up any life, far down below.

The vast urban sprawl known as Kabul was one thing. With the swarm of mule carts, droves of unwary pedestrians, and motorcycles carrying up to four men at a time, it seemed almost impossible not to run over a kid on some days. But—out in the pristine nothingness—my eyes searched for movement.

The first flight from Dubai to Kabul; the smile on my face couldn't be chiseled off with a jackhammer. It had been five years since I had gotten boots on the ground in foreign hostile territory. A few weeks into the gig a rocket attack outside Camp Sullivan reactivated that same smile. It aimed for all the warm bodies, but no joy. I wasn't technically a warrior anymore—but there was still a war.

Now on my fifth or sixth flight into Kabul, its smog and dust was officially in my arteries. No life down there this time, I thought. Maybe next time, if I keep a sharp eye out.

The plane coming in for its landing, local nationals arms up; praise Allah for a safe flight. I thumbed some old mag pouches in my carry-on. Staying with me from the combat days, they were back in action. If they had a life of their own, I reckon they would've had more to say to me than most people I left back home. Maybe some old times, coming again, old friend.

We land. We exit. We link up with our contacts and convoy to our geographic footprint in that great shithole. The little jailhouse gym echoes the thumps and clangs from within. A local truck driver working in the camp, our pusher man, starts taking our orders for Anavar, Clenbuterol, and Viagra.

20

WORSHIPPING THE GODS OF WAR AND WINE

Many of them have sought my counsel because they feel guilty, but when I ask them why, they say they feel bad because they haven't had a chance to fire their weapons. They worry that they haven't done their jobs as marines. I've had to counsel them that if you don't have to shoot somebody, that's a good thing. The zeal these young men have for killing surprises me.

—Chaplain assigned to 1st Recon Battalion
(Evan Wright's *Generation Kill*)

But forget not the reckless warrior souls.
Despite their roughness,
Let us take a moment to allot compassion and praise.
For every harm that threatens your gods
Must first face the warriors,
With their wayward ways.

THERE ARE MANY THAT simply go to war to die. Why not just commit suicide? Good question. Because death, for those who actively seek it in combat, is not the ultimate goal; rather it is the tool used to achieve it. Myself, and I would come to find out several others, extracted ourselves from the civilian world, feeling far from happy about the droll, obscure box we had treaded water in. To us sad, sullen few, death in combat seemed to serve as some form of validation of what was otherwise a trite and meaningless existence.

Coming from every failure known to man and his society, a combat troop, ascending a steep hill to reload the only heavy gun, risking all to keep the fight alive and his comrades breathing, shot in the spine and through the heart, tumbles to the muddy base to die, eyes up and open, a complete and actualized being. This actualization, whether real or not, an illusion or not, is perceived as unable to be achieved in the world in which this lost soul had come from.

I considered the possibility of dying in combat to be the greatest death ever, and to some maybe it is. Much of that changed for me, however, the first time I saw someone involuntarily take that plunge. Death quickly lost all romance, and soon became the quiet, impersonal vacuum left after a bloody surprise.

However, years after I left the military, I learned of a great death—one that still resonates, and would be the source of many midnight-hour ruminations while studying in London.

———◦———

MY MID-TWENTIES WILL FOREVER be chalked up to a socio-psychological wandering, full-coma induced, in what can only be called "my experiment as a cop" phase. I wasn't a very good one— by conventional standards—but there was more than one boy in blue who smiled and rolled his shoulders when I backed him to quell a rowdy noise complaint.

NOTE: Southern Ghetto. Ghetto means the poor people who live there happen to be black; get over it, it's not a value judgement. Central Florida, the "I-4 Corridor," the source of media crown jewels like Zimmerman and Casey Anthony, is also one of the most relocation-prone places in the country. Yet, wedged sturdily in the transience, in a small, poor, nook exists a hearty culture that has been there since Osceola was asked to sign and Flagler was making his name on the coast. Sustenance farming and fishing still rules the day—superb fishermen and owners of small, mixed gardens that grow almost year round in the Land of Flowers. The old Southern African American world. Peaceful, almost serene—until, that is, the twenty-first century inevitably reared its stiff and ugly head. The infamous demographic—black America, ages sixteen to thirty-four—where some energetically gave weight to just about every negative stereotype you'd hear out of the tooth-rot mouths at a Klan meeting. Apparently geared up with long-praised and highly illegal tools and traits, they would climb up the ladder to reach what a few rappers and athletes gloated about. Would—or would die trying.

In this southern ghetto, a stolen car on twenty-six-inch fake gold rims could be seen careening down a dirt road. Chickens egressing for their lives, a dice game ruined, and a grandfather screaming as the pink Cadillac passes the front porch, "You know yo mamma gonna kill you, boy!"

Trying to catch someone there reminded me of working in Iraq again. Except here, I would have been in a shit-ton more trouble if I cooked off a few rounds in the general direction of someone I was after. Tribalism bled out (a more primitive yet emotionally invested form of rule) into the current laws so many others from the north side of that town clung to for dear life. A man wanted for murder in Alabama, hiding in the southern ghetto of my jurisdiction, would quickly be absorbed by the community and vanish into the closest house. There was a local unification that was confrontational to my efforts, our efforts.

Yet, this two-story town had trusted me, giving me a vest, a gun, and a few books to maintain good order and discipline on these streets…my streets, my forty-hour-a-week southern ghetto.

It was in this place I learned of a death that rang a peculiar, awe-invoking reverence, so daring, primal, and simple that no matter which way I ever tried to muck it up with melancholy, it still rang its wide-grinned ring.

I HAD RECEIVED A call on the radio about a car crash on the edge of town. An isolated group of houses sat across from what was then a massive construction site. Out of this tiny neighborhood, the city had paved a new road. Black, smooth, and straight, this road came out from the hovel to greet an adjoining road at a final downhill.

A drag race had gone bad, real bad. A grandfather and his grandson decided to race for…well, for the fucking hell of it apparently.

There was an accident. I was not first on scene, but I got to see enough. The old-timer had lost control and his car went into a ditch. It went into a ditch and that is where he would die, right there—grandson out of the car, wide-eyed, seeing the full results of the race.

My grandfathers: one died a feeble shell of his former self, too brain-dead to even know it, and the other with a BAL of over .40. That grandson, however, the dragster who lived, will walk through life knowing that his grandfather was a breed not so commonly found. Too alive to make it to the nursing home and too hard to go out with a whimper.

It is easy to imagine the moments leading up to it all. A young gun and his abnormally spry grandfather belted into their beasts. Eyes set straight ahead, revving their engines—and then they're off. Tires squealing and thick, black smoke from the rubber and the demons exorcised from the rusty exhausts are the only things remaining from where they were just a moment before. First gear, second gear, third gear, and maybe fourth, the relatives fly down the tarmac, the old man's black knuckles turn white on the steering wheel as the grandson yells, "I have the coolest granddad…ever!" Their vision needles to the space directly in front of the hood and they see the summit of the road just ahead. Then something goes awry. Grandpa's arthritis and glaucoma pound his youthfulness back to harsh reality; his arms, once strong, can't take the forceful vibrations of the bucking steering wheel. He loses control, and into a ditch the Buick plows. He could have become the pre-rigor mortis, risk-intolerant drone that many of his species opt for settling for, but no, not this dragster. Grandpa went out worshipping a different set of gods.

———◦◦◦———

THAT WRECK WAS ONE of the few things I remember with any real clarity about the two and a half years in which I slogged through life as a police officer. I had receded into *that* uniform because at the time it seemed a logical progression. Carrying a gun was my marketable skill, my only one as far as I was concerned.

It was in those days that I would spend an entire nightshift playing spider solitaire or talking to girls on the phone. Or maybe I would find myself in a store, where I had to explain to some fourteen-year-old, just sprouting hair on his balls, that if he ever bumped against my gun side again (to impress some girl who looked like the result of Barbie getting pregnant by a crack pipe) that I would bounce his little forehead across every tile in the place.

Or maybe deal with the derelict asking to be taken to the state-sanctioned facility used to house those who are going through withdrawal, contemplating suicide, or the like. Those street urchins usually wanted to be admitted for the free pills, and even cutely memorized verbatim the whole spiel about "without help I believe I am a threat to myself and others." They were mildly entertaining at best, yet a bit caustic to a state budget.

I had offered one my gun once, to kill itself of course, and of course it did not. Committing the unrepentable sin of officer safety, I handed it my issued Glock-21. I could articulate later that it wrestled me to the ground and seized the weapon. It was short, bald, and troll-like, and under the awning of the gas station, the neon flickered in the sweat beading off its sooty skin. Its eyes rolled up to meet mine, its face showing curious disbelief.

My lieutenant appeared out of nowhere. I snatched back my service weapon, as its momentary possessor also reacted with an abrupt start. We both looked like kids getting caught with a porno mag, looking at the approaching authority figure with that collective "Oh shit." Ruining the moment, my superior told me what he wanted done. Alas, it was Baker Acted, and I was deprived a most coveted "stateside kill," even if by proxy.

Off the clock, in those days, the outlook was just as simmering and antisocial.

How the people of my jurisdiction would have writhed in horror: The cop in long sleeves taking the crash report at

2:00 p.m.; at 2:00 a.m...a rifle against the couch, Glock-19, and flashlight on the coffee table, maybe a beer too. The flashlight was for if they cut the power; the pistol in case the rifle had a squib load. Images from a DVD, playing once-heralded works that had long settled into obscurity, flickered on the TV as a rogue leaning slowly seeped its way out of the public servant.

In law enforcement, I was undeniably a black sheep. I was unmarried, had twenty-plus tattoos, had a tanning bed in my home (closet fag, as it was to be whispered), and worst of all I had come from the GWOT generation. This meant I had no way of kidding myself how utterly boring 99 percent of law enforcement was.

When someone has watched a MK-19 decimate a house, or a fire team efficiently utilize some bounding overwatch to break contact, or to zero in on a crowd with an M4 and open it up, busting some scumbag for his ninety-second crack arrest just doesn't get your dick hard. Maybe worst of all, the military mindset had been marketed to law enforcement, which resulted in countless cops referring to themselves as "sheep dogs" and/or quoting that thing about "—rough men willing to," conveniently ignoring that they were twenty pounds overweight, had never been shot at, and weren't going to a GP[68] tent later, but a furnished home with air-conditioning. Nevertheless, I was neck-deep in; lesbians with a bizarre axe to grind, sheltered social rejects with a developed vendetta, the morbidly obese, and the thorn in my eye...the "warrior cop"...gear strapped to him like a GI Joe as he embarked on his crusade.

The incessant comparisons of military to law enforcement (apparently because both involve guns) were almost too hard to take at times. Both were fighting wars, damn you! In the ultimate gesture of passive-aggressive Fuckyouism, I would always take a

---

68   General purpose: large tents usually used to house numerous military personnel

different stripper to their esoteric, frustrated, and married-too-long gatherings. Upon my approach once, a wife of a SWAT guy took her child by the hand and scurried away; the point was getting across. The high irony was that they were forever ignorant to the dark and rough appendages of the warrior culture. Squeaky clean and politically correct, obligatory trademarks of professional law enforcement, they had no place in a fighting hole or bullet-riddled Humvee, yet the comparisons were made. But comparing law enforcement to the military is like comparing a trapeze artist to commercial fishermen because they both use nets.

Warrior semantics examined:

The term *warrior* is thrown around as clumsily as *love* and *hate*. Warriors for: ending poverty, marijuana law reform, animal rights, gay and lesbian rights, equal pay in the workplace, equal time in the classroom, a tobacco-free state, selling beer on Sunday. Warriors in business, education, and a plethora of others. The commonality, of course, is fighting for or against something. But a radical twist is thus: it's been my experience that not even all soldiers are real warriors. Perhaps more interesting still, not all warriors are soldiers, as soldier is commonly understood.

> *The army is still rotten with such as thee.*
> *With professionals such as thee.*
>
> —Ernest Hemingway (Gomez),
> *For Whom the Bell Tolls*

> *A warrior who does not conform to military discipline nor comply with social conventions is not a soldier…such an armed outlaw is either an adventurer or a psychopath.*
>
> —From an anonymous source, retrieved from "Verbal Shrapnel"

The soldier is in the vein of the cop; uniformed executer of government directive. They are the white blood cells in an intricate immune system. Important, certainly, and a necessary evil at the very worst.

The warrior, by contrast, comes to the fight from an abstract point, from a place of identity that runs far deeper than a job title, a salary, and a simplistic war to wage. The warrior is a blade, to be used to defend the helpless or to lop off their heads. Most important of all, the warrior is a warrior even without a war. Conflicts often change, but DNA and the spirit rarely do.

So where do these fundamental differences come from? Looking to the antiquated ways in which humanity place cause and purpose seems to help.

Insert the gods:

The cop and the professional soldier—when viewed correctly as an occupation-first, passion-second—worship the civil-centric municipal pantheon. These are people who believe in a certain social structure and will do much to nobly defend it. From this perspective, gods have emerged in human history to reflect these ideas and interests. Gods of harvest, fertility, wealth, commerce, and even law itself. The human animal has made certain social arrangements work, certain contracts among and within the crowd. From these "working class" gods, sectarian traditions, priorities, and rituals have emerged.

The working man from a working family, plowing the fields all day—fields protected by law from thieves and vandals—comes home on cobbled streets funded by taxation. Local ordinance allows this man to travel safely and with good order to his home. His wife, done cooking the dinner for his large family, greets him. Some god of fertility blesses the family; there is not a sick child as they are fruitful in their multiplication. As the weekend beckons, they hop in the cart and make to the village square, where music and beer greet the denizens of this small, industrious, thriving, and totally boring place.

Across a small sea, however, there dwell others. An island, large and jagged, was not placed in the correct location to develop farming the way the municipal-god-worshippers were able to.

The flora here is scant—sporadic trees and shrubberies that all look ill. Geological factors make vertical cliff walls in the dark, dank draws between the stony fingers of their Earth God—some sleeping ogre, perhaps. In conjunction with all that, the wind howls in its trapped spaces, as it tries in vain to return to the sea; the myth of trolls (howling) in these places is born.

Farming will not work on this island, not at a rate to feed its populace, like the industrious peasant neighbors across the wild sea. However, the flora has created the perfect world for mega-fauna to develop. Bear and Hawk and Elk and Wolf reign supreme as the other forest critters scurry in the damp darkness and the sick shrubbery. The people of this island have their gods too, made from the same sociological necessity, rooted in geographical causation as the municipal-god-worshippers.

Here on this island, however, predators, sharp falls, and the cold lick of sea wind make childbearing much different than is the case for the farmers. Only a few make it to five years old, thus emplacing an idealism in this community: the importance of physical strength. Defending their kin from hungry wolves and bears emplaces the idealism of combat efficiency. A wild love for drink and its very own god emblazon the attitude. They see the world as full of danger, and the gods they worship give them what they need (courage, weapons, levity) and are of course embodiments of such, as seen by their statues, in their bearskin-rug-laden shrines.

In time, a leader with his small horde of wild men hunts the bears almost to extinction. Same fate for the wolves. The trolls are bravely searched for but never found. Order and tactics oil themselves into ritual and martial tradition. These island men begin to look to the sea they'd always fished. Voyage looms. The gods gave them the bravery to beat back the beasts and earn total dominion over their land. They, dressed in the regalia of bear claws, take to shipbuilding. There are just no more bears left to kill.

One day, farmers worshipping harvest and law look up to see an approaching armada. Whatever defense they have, they hope it will withstand those who worship the gods of war and wine.

How is this relevant in present day?

To make a long story very, very short, take the case above; strikingly similar to numerous cases throughout history. Max Weber (as well as many priests who gratefully sighed as raiding became viewed as a violation of God's law) would agree; given enough time, cultures merge, whether through cooperation or total or partial conquest. This means their gods merge too— which is theological talk for the merging of ideals. What we are left with is a synthesis. The values of both are alive in what is now normally a nation.

The USA holds such a synthesis. The value differences in people are stupendous. Next to a warrior soul in the checkout line stands a cog in the wheel, terrified of life, helmet-fastened farmer soul—the living antithesis of the people they'd consider, and rightfully so, to be a reckless threat to their revered tranquility.

But in the information age—typed to new heights by soft, fat fingers—the very dispositions so feared, so scoffed at, and given such a wide birth serve municipality in the moments it is most threatened. But it's only for a limited time—then comes the reemergence of mayhem. The jail cells swell as the peace horn sings.

Farmers and warriors, farmer souls and warrior souls[69]. The cop and the professional soldier, there to stop bullets and prevent the life they love from being altered to an unwashable ugliness. A different breed of citizen, from a different emotional place, however, emerges every time the drum is beat. Out of the city streets, the suburbs, the wooden hills, from churches, farms and bars and gyms, construction sites, plea deals, and offices... the Warriors do come. Much with the same intentions as the more timid souls who stand next to them in the ranks, but with one crucial additional ingredient: a desire to kill as palpable as blood itself.

The moral question: is the Warrior...*good*?

Generally speaking, in literature, spanning across all cultures, from the days of painting in caves to blogs with hashtags, the human mind has loved to categorize and grandly distinguish what we refer to as Good and Evil. The Good Guy: some Roy Rogers-type sheriff on a white horse. The Bad Guy: the unsavory, unshaven man scurrying like the rat he is. The hero versus the monster. The one-dimensional, moral monolith taking on the thing with the foul name and foul appearance. In the mythos of every culture, there seems to be some force of good, manifest in a human agent, doing battle with the embodiment of the pitfalls and calamities of the human experience.

---

69   There is a third category, one well worth mentioning: the professional soldier-warrior hybrid, the one who possesses the innate characteristics of the Warrior, and who chooses the stability of military life as a career in the vein of the professional soldier. However, there is a distinction between those who see the stability of the paycheck and those who see a calling. Sure, the stability is taken into consideration, stated clearly from any professional soldier I have ever spoken to, but to the professional soldier-warrior hybrid, these rare men that nations are forever indebted to, the insulating blanket of stability comes in miles behind the passion for the job itself

Considering rape, murder, drought, disease, flooding, food poisoning, fire, earthquakes, snakebites, betrayal, joy, love, friendship, fidelity, and pleasures of song, dance, and social cohesion, it's not shocking to understand why the pragmatic human brain neatly categorizes such things, as well as assigns agency and causation to such. And what is important to realize is the aforementioned features are applicable to all in the human experience, no matter what pantheon they choose to abide by.

However, that dog only hunts so well. It's not a secret to many, but anyone ever called a "hero" for doing anything involving holding a weapon knows the hero is multidimensional, as is the hero's thought process, intentions, and overall moral makeup.

Not all who go to war for their society actually go to war *for* their society. There are those who put on a uniform to execute the urges that wail from inside the deepest of places. Whether to die or to facilitate death, the warrior is beyond the confines of the war effort itself.

Cops, culture, and hodgepodge theology; checked off. Now the closer:

Do they really think we all gave a shit about the Iraqi or Afghan people...or them? There is a truth out there, clawing just under the surface, that may cause a lot of startled citizens to take down the yellow ribbons for good and hang a smaller American flag outside their front door. We—the reluctant heroes of the country songs and candlelit vigils—wanted to kick ass, and that is just shorthand for wanting to kill. To see it happen. To live through it. To answer our very own call of the wild. To know it could have been you but it was the other guy; likely on the same morbid quest.

How does that sit in the stomachs of the churches who sent group prayers to their brave, presumably Christian, and of course...nationalistic soldiers? How does that sit to the news personalities who described the soldier as "scared to death" while standing some post for an obscure better tomorrow? How does that sit to the third-grade teacher, married to the god-fearing plumber, who wrote to the deployed soldier "you're a hero, making the sacrifices you are"?

The news that surrounds war is categorically grim. Seeing young people ripped from their prime of life, just sprouting out from the adolescent soil. Some left a maimed relic of themselves. The image of selfless citizens dying is hard for many to swallow.

Bring now the tidings that will either free them from that horror, or will plunge them down deeper into a realization even more unsettling: their heroic ranks are teeming with an ancient breed they dare not imagine. Dare not imagine when putting that push in the diaphragm at the ballgame when the singer concludes, "Braaaaaave." Dare not imagine when they stare at the family portrait of the infantryman who turned family man but still has that something behind his eyes.

21

BARROOM ENCOUNTERS

SUMMER 2004

An aged and learned perspective, I find clear, when listening
to the eighteen-year-old at the bar ramble on in drunken
celebratory vigor that he is joining the military. The usual
bevy of impostors gloat of being "special forces." The beer
churns in my gut, and I think.

Who are these young men who join? The excited proclaimer
demands the visual of semi-directionless youth, riddled in
testosterone and without family who own much land, public
offices, or an Ivy League sweater. The lower rung of our
socioeconomic hierarchy, ready to snap to—for God, for
country, for meaning, for the girl who cheated and for the
guy who bullied, and for the Montgomery GI Bill.

Now how I see the obligatory praise the ruling class
bestows upon us. The need to convince the prisoners of the
West that we are the best and the brightest.

But forget not and take the moment to recall the lordship
forged within our own existence. The joke is not on the
fighter, who becomes lord of this world with the fine motor
skill of a single trigger squeeze.

Set to embark; the retaking of Fallujah. Word had trickled down that our unit was to have a role in a battle that was sure to go down in history. Operators had been bouncing back and forth a healthy amount of speculation—who had heard what, when, and from whom. The mix of excitement, anticipation, and anxiety manifested itself in different ways, and the preparatory phase could be as unique as the individuals experiencing it. One of the more entertaining collective responses was the throwing out of porn, lest the following:

> *Dear Mrs. Johnson, your son's possessions will be arriving via USPS on the 14th.*

> *On the 14th, a bereaved mother, still smelling like the coach seat from the flight back from Arlington, opens a tightly sealed cardboard box, fully loaded with DOD stickers and maybe even a letter from his Command. Under a skim surface of T-shirts is the entire series collections of* Cumback Pussy, Buttfaced, *and* Sugar Walls.

It was an irksome, potential reality that crossed many minds, mine included. Legend has it that on the night of our departure, a particular marine, not slotted for our deployment and known for his acquiring nature, spelunked the battalion Dumpster to wallow in the cornucopia that was his to claim.

My reaction was probably the typical one. I realized I was very capable of dying and accepted it, accepted the fear, and went forward with it. I had a dream one night that I was being hunted by some primitive people in the darkness and ended up getting caught then burned alive. Soon after this dream, I got one of my largest tattoos: a ghastly scene, caught in its own happening, cleverly illustrating *Death On The Brain*: the proverb of that era.

When not at the gym, or on the range, or getting drunk out of my mind, I focused on poetry. Evenly dispersed into two categories— the realization of my own looming death and the pure, bestial hope to kill others.

Many are taken aback by the mere thought of the latter. However, when someone volunteers for ground combat units eleven months after 9/11, then claws and bites their way into schools to maximize their lethality, what could ultimately motivate such a person, if not to kill?

To be clear, the complexity of killing as a motivation requires a sensitive approach. I personally never considered the act of killing to be the pot of gold at the end of the rainbow. Rather, I looked at it as an essential step toward the ultimate goal: to be tested, and the blighting out of another hostile life was the ultimate test and trophy. I had already tested my mind and body in what was arguably some of the most intense training available in the entirety of the Department of Defense. Prolific attrition rates didn't lie. However, I had yet to see how I was to react to being under enemy fire. Would I duck quickly enough? Would I return fire soon enough? How would I react to being shot? Would I feel it? What would my reaction be to watching my buddy next to me get the back of his head cleaned out by a 7.62 round? These were things I desperately needed to know, and the annihilation of some mujahideen was simply a means to an end.

After our rather hilarious and, at times, confusing predeployment work-up, we were let loose on leave. I was back in Florida and found myself a bar with a mechanical bull. I insisted on wearing a Recon shirt. I wanted what many young gunslingers want(ed): women to ogle and men to fear you. Instead, however, my shirt resulted in free beers from patriotic onlookers as I rode the machine over and over.

Finally tired of the bull and finding myself a bit thirsty, I wedged myself up against the bar. Later that same night, the people I went with would prove to be the greatest entertainment of all. One guy, a day out of shoulder surgery, had to defend his bewildered wife from a drunk New Yorker who was nearly seven feet tall. Another guy, who would have been useful during said defensive, decided instead to initiate a vicious and relentless attack on a young Puerto Rican couple. I remember the guy trying hard, and doing quite well, to act like he wasn't terrified.

At the bar I caught some middle-aged man leering at me. I looked down at my own arm, seeing the USMC tattoo that was billboarded right at him. My eyes moved between us, hovering across the bar's surface, and then crawled up to finally meet his stare. His sharp face was curiously set, his dark-pebble eyes squinting at me. Dressed in mostly black with a goatee of successfully encroached gray, he took a drink, "How long you been in?" he asked.

"Two years," I replied.

"So what do you do?"

At this point, the combination of free beer, bull riding, and the thawing-out erection from a groping MILF in cat glasses had me walking tall. Chest puffed out a bit, I kind of cocked my head to one side to respond, "This," while simultaneously exposing the word "RECON" above the tattoo of a razor on my right wrist.

He stared at it like he'd just watched the first few seconds of a cheesy rerun, then turned the channel.

"Why the hell would you do that?" he snapped.

I'd never received this type of reaction. Normally it was stuff like "Oh, Recon, yeah I played that game," or "My brother is in the ROTC at our school and is slotted for Delta Force," or "Is that like a Navy SEAL?" His reaction, however, was proprietary of some sort of experience, I could tell.

He must have seen the look on my face.

"I'm sorry, son. Didn't mean it that way. It's just, why not get a skill you can actually use in the real world, like a rotary wing mechanic, something you can really use?" He pointed to my tattoo. "Besides be an assassin."

What transpired, my official rebuttal, was surely a drunken and wordy explanation, sunk in existentialism. We pulled our stools closer and he told me of his time in Vietnam as a marine grunt, and I recall him abruptly sounding like a gym coach. "Try not to get shot—it hurts."

The conversation came to its natural end, as those types of talks always seem to do.

I had to try to find the blonde woman in glasses, but before departing he shook my hand and said, "Good luck overseas, son."

As the years have passed, I have assigned a lot of value to that night. In part due to his cold nature, that type of John Wayne stoic masculinity that still lingers in twenty-first-century perceptions of manhood. However, I believe the reason that man is burned into my head is twofold: one, his ominous declaration regarding employability, and two, he is but one of two barroom encounters in all my life when the man behind the big stories and big ideas was actually what he claimed to be, determined by intense mutual vetting that is akin to dogs circling the other, butt-sniffing in full effect.

22

E & E

RIP (RECON INDOCTRINATION PLATOON), referred to sometimes as RTP (Recon Training Platoon), was an in-house school of sorts that has since gone the way of the wooly mammoth. The acronym is something, yet again, contested as swiped from the Army Rangers. Which in this case is a likelihood, considering we used Ranger Beads, Ranger Joe protractors, and so forth. But despite some barstool razzing, this is really a nonissue. One will notice that inane service rivalry dissipates quickly in the special operations community. Much like the willful stupidity surrounding rival high school football teams, hollow inner-service competition is for the very young (or new), the moronic, and the recruiters.

RIP was unique in the Marine Corps. ARS made recon marines, but something was needed to make students ready for ARS. Due to a need to provide ARS with men physically and mentally capable of graduating, RIP was a school before a school—an initial, preparatory step in a challenging two-step process. This made RIP a school hosted entirely by a unit, with unit staff and unit funding. 1st Recon Battalion would have their RIP, as would 2nd, as would the Force companies. Operators from the teams were the cadre, most without a day's training in formal instructor techniques.

When RIP existed, it was up to the Reconnaissance community to groom its own candidates, and do so in ways the community saw fit.

One thing learned quickly in Recon (and I'm willing to wage the same is true in similar outfits): while certain traditions remain intact, most things, beckoning to the whims of whatever branch and the accordion effect of DOD, mutate sporadically. Recon marines from 1997, 2007, and 2017 would/will tell very different stories regarding vetting, whereabouts of entire units, the nature of Recon as an MOS, and so forth. Specifically with regards to the turn-of-the-millennium era, RIP weeded out the weak and then prepped the worthy, as a means to have the highest number of ARS graduates possible. RIP consisted of rigorous physical training, both on land and in the water, enough so as to expose the deficiencies in any Rope who had any.

RIP students were "Ropes." One of the oldest, long-standing traditions and skillsets in Marine Recon is rope work. From paddle wrapping to HRST[70] to repelling, recon marines are technically proficient in knots. An iconic symbol is the twelve-foot rope, seen in black and white photos of the Vietnam era, and recruiting posters spanning decades. The RIP student wore these 3.7 meters of skilled heritage almost like suspenders, or diagonally on the torso the way a beauty pageant contestant wears her sash.

In addition to the physical conditioning, advanced patrolling techniques and community familiarization made up the bulk of the training. There was one event that tied all these elements together: the escape and evasion run, or E&E.

From the perspective of the outsider who unwittingly stumbled upon such a thing, it would look to them as if a disembodied remnant of a military formation was running with a lot of gear on. They wouldn't be wrong. The idea is very simple:

---

70   Helicopter rope suspension training

run an extremely long distance with your combat load, and run like your life depends on it. The reason such a training event exists is deeply rooted in both historical and theoretical contexts.

Certain military occupations are known as *high risk of capture*. Any job involving being a pilot or crew in an aircraft, as well as any operator in the Spec Ops community, fills the vast majority of this category. The reasoning for the former is rather simple: getting shot down or crashing. For the latter, it is due to key features of the job, namely being behind enemy lines, covert in nature, and small in numbers with little support. Marine Recon was particularly subject to these potentialities because we were built from the ground up as an information-gathering entity. Direct Action (gunfights inside of buildings), infantry-based patrolling (gunfights outside of buildings), and a hodgepodge of other assets were all feats capably performed by the covert elements, even though the stated primary purpose of Marine Recon was to get in somewhere undetected, collect information undetected, and get the fuck out undetected. If they were compromised the extreme last resort was to *run through the jungle*. From the point of enemy contact to friendly lines, whether one mile or one hundred, the E&E was when the shit hit the tail rotor.

The two most famous cases of E&Es being conducted are Jack Sillito, a British SAS[71] trooper who covered around ninety miles in the Sahara Desert during WWII, and Chris Ryan, also SAS, who astonishingly outdid Jack by almost one hundred miles during the First Gulf War. These cases are rare, but uniformly intense. This act requires a gritty fortitude that cannot be assumed, only proven. Therefore, a monumental training event awaited anyone who wished to be one of these clandestine men of the shadows.

---

71   Special Air Service

Toward the end of RIP, the cadre would provide a week of back-to-back patrolling. This was to give Ropes a valuable experience. ARS contained that extensive and harshly graded patrol phase. If Ropes were going to go to ARS well prepared, then a simulation of graded events was crucial to overall success.

The training areas of Camp Lejeune are some of the most heavily vegetated, bug and humidity infested, featureless terrain the military can provide within the United States. If you can land navigate successfully in Camp Lejeune and/or Stone Bay, you can land navigate anywhere.

In the cold of mid-December, teams of six to eight Ropes were assembled. Billets were assigned: the point man, team leader, radio operator, assistant radio operator, slack man, and assistant team leader. Add one or two RIP cadre, and the whole gang would insert into the bush. Thus began the RIP patrol week.

What followed were several days of breaking horizontal canopy—walls of twigs and vines so thick an exhausted Rope could, and did, lie up against it, full body weight and laden ruck, and still appear to be standing. The patrols, all with various objectives, bled into each other; the only things changing were the billets within the team and the faces of the instructor. Sleep was sparse and mold in the mouth grew, as did the collective weariness. After a handful of missions, spills into ditches at 3:00 a.m., and exhilarating confirmations of pace counts, the final gathering coalesced sometime in the early night.

My team was one of the last to arrive. At a large, cleared-out intersection of tank and Humvee trails, connecting willowy like an octopus, the other teams were sitting in quiet, single files. A mumble from a familiar voice breaking over the diesel putter of a lone Humvee, staged ominously like an olive drab hearse. Slight, jerky movement from guys in the files, adjusting the placement of canteens against the hip bones or looking over shoulders to try to make out what team was coming in. Everyone knew what was coming next. The pause prior to its commencement was recuperative and full of that nervous silence that occupies moments before jumping out of planes, watching the panties come down for the first time, or sizing up the other guys in the parking lot—knowing just one word from your group's mouthpiece will start the spilling of the blood.

"Everyone on your feet." The command came from some distant instructor; down a sandy trail I knew we were about to tackle, and for a very long time. For some reason, as if a composer had waved his baton, a few animals starting yelling and chanting all kinds of shit. It was going to hurt, it was going to test, but that was why the morale was at a point of lunacy. Those who were there, in those files, were on some sort of drug.

After years of working with such men, it was made clear beyond doubt that what makes a unit *Spec Ops* is not the gear, nor the titles, nor even its history. It wasn't just the runs, or the vetting—it was everything. These men by most accounts were logical beings—staring more than once at me during some proclamation that buoyed me to the peculiar—yet these same men put themselves in extraordinary situations time and time again. Where the country thanked us for doing what so many couldn't, we surmised it was that they wouldn't, and we sat, ran, and eventually shot, grateful for a world so brutal. The point may be distilled most efficiently in the gunfight; the sheer terror, the heart-stopping fear of being burrowed through by the zings and cracks around you...yet also the strange inner peace, the calling answered, and answered well.

The run began. For the next several hours a group of about thirty ran up and down every trail in an area covering a couple dozen grid squares. North, south, whatever. As the blood pumped, any recollection of direction was lost, replaced with the simplicity of a cattle drive.

The purpose was to keep going until someone somewhere, way up ahead or in the trailing Humvee, said to stop. Beyond the obvious, there was an additional incentive: the rumored consequence of falling out, the most shameful reminder of one's own weakness. The RIP corpsmen, a SARC[72] who would later die in Afghanistan, wielded the *Silver Bullet*. If a Rope was left by the pack, it was articulable that he was a "heat case." He would be pinned down and buggered by a robust, weapons-grade thermometer, it was rumored, and the event would go into one's medical record, which only bolstered the dire need to avoid it.

After hours and miles, exhaustion claimed me, as it did the drunk monkey running in front of me.

Good old Chris—Bullet, who'd be my future Myrtle Beach, bouncer-fighting cohort, swooped in by my side; a psychotic athlete in my ear, envious of the drunk monkey.

"I am so fuckin' jealous of him right now, dude," Chris said. "He's in, like, another total fuckin' mind state."

I struggled to just toss one leg in front of the other, barely on my feet and avoiding potholes; almost completely shrouded in the darkness of what had to be around 3:00 a.m.

"He's having to dig deeper, bro," Chris said in an envious chant. "He's digging deeper than us. He is going *allll* the way—"

I managed to swing my bone-weary face toward him, nearly toppling over in the process. Looking into those eyes I could see there was jet fuel pumping in his veins. Chris, looking into mine, saw I was going into whatever place the drunken monkey was already dwelling

---

72   Special Amphibious Reconnaissance Corpsmen

Watching the back of Chris's ruck dart ahead, my eyes rolled up to the sky. The stars swarmed and danced—white bugs on the surface of the black lake.

We are a way for the cosmos to know itself.

—Carl Sagan

If we [humans] are the universe contemplating itself, then the universe may be one dumb motherfucker.

—Recon Marine, sunk in cosmology

And up into the black lake I fell.

A sun explodes, the heavier elements form, inorganic matter turns to organic life, a smattering of a billion years or so of evolutionary biology, thousands of generations of hominids... then me, born in 1983 to two peasants, one praying and the other likely drunk. Emerged from the stuff of stars, never having asked for any of this, yet this I was given. This short, fierce, beautiful time, in which I, as have others, decided to face the cosmos' adversity, thus draped in the darker shades and often dwelling in the harshness of the human experience.

Hydrogen, carbon, a bit of iron and some zinc, now running in mud-covered boots, breathing heavy. Other masses of the same clutter will their way to the finish line, our barracks pond—some living on the wind, others teeter-tottering on broken stumps.

Coming back from the *in* and regrasping the *out*, voices of the RIP cadre on high, we were ordered to stand shoulder to shoulder on a long edge of the pond, frozen over in a thin film of dirty ice and slush. The pond, shaped like a maggot, had a Rope covering every foot of its bayside. A senior instructor was speaking, but I couldn't make out the words. I heard my heart beating, others panting, and the cracks and gurgles of the pond ice's edge being broken by boots looking for a footing.

For reasons unidentifiable, myself and Chris, who had found his way next to me, were violently jockeying for position. Shoves, pulls, and growls—so out of nowhere that a RIP cadre's "you guys are fuckin' crazy" resonated in our ears; letting each other go in a snarling impasse.

It was about 4:30 a.m., an hour before most of the Marine Corps would be expected to awake, and about the time I would be going to bed every night a decade later.

"What do you want to be, RIP?!" Cholo yelled from the second deck of the barracks.

"Recon!" answered the mob.

"What do you want to beeeeee, RIP?!"

"Recon!!"

"Cross over."

Into the air leaped a Rope, suspended for just a moment in the witchy twilight of the barracks lights, and then dove into the bursting ice. We followed. Under, over, and through the ice, sometimes swimming, other times at a crawl. The ice sheet was annihilated into fragments of pale muck.

Standing on the other side—signifying the run's completion, the pond was the night's final task. The group dive; a Fuck You to anything that could pain a mortal man.

23

ON THE RIVERS OF BABYLON

Every morning someone wakes wanting to kill you. When you walk down the street, they are waiting, and you want to kill them, too.

—Brian Mockenhaupt, *I Miss Iraq. I Miss My Gun. I Miss My War.*

FALL 2004

W HAT WOULD END UP being the Marine Corps' bloodiest battle since the Vietnam War, the second battle of Fallujah, aka Operation Phantom Fury, had begun. Days earlier, there was a feeling in the air that I had never felt prior, and not even the remotest replication of after. The volume was down on everything. For me, at least, it reminded me of walking around in a silent movie, just with a few drab industrial and desert colors. The camp laundry had a list of units that were unable to use their services, and we knew these were the ones that were to be staging north of the city.

If the wind could have talked, somehow expressing the collective consciousness blanketing the area, it would have most likely said, "You joined for this, motherfucker. Your fear, your uncertainty...none of it matters now. Some powerful people far away want you in that city and your ass is going in there."

Several people expressed how much sense it made to just drop a tactical nuke on the city, but the war effort required something of a more discriminate resolution.

Initiated, peculiarly, just two days before the Marine Corps birthday, my platoon found itself not only outside the city, but sitting in the damn farmlands south of the war. 2D Recon was tasked with surrounding the bottom edge of Fallujah; my company—Alpha Company—in sight of the Euphrates River's northern shore. My company, particularly my platoon, was to intercept any reinforcements that would try to support the fortified insurgency within. There was a settled, collective disappointment among us, knowing the military had pumped a lot of money into all our training yet we were not fighting in the city with the infantry units. The infantry; groups of men so pissed off and ready to kill that covertly entering a neighboring infantry unit's battle space was far more terrifying than breaching a house to potentially shoot a man in a sandy dress.

Yeah, grunts are yut-yut as hell and basically equivalent to battered housewives in that for some inexplicable reason they continually reenlist to undergo more beratement while in the rear and deployed, but those poor abused souls are like ants when it comes to war. Everything in their path will be devoured.

—Recon Marine and private contractor extraordinaire

More than just their willingness to fight was the reality of their continual injection into the most violent of places. That is the truest honor of the infantry; the casual, expendable nature of their existence—and I never had greater respect for them than the moment I realized this, south of Fallujah.

More than one person expressed painful discontent that we were to watch for potential river crossers instead of fighting building to building, as our marine forefathers had done in Hue City in 1968. In fact, it was Hue City that the fight was compared to, by our own CO, just before kicking off for the operation. To hear the gunfire, know that potentially the greatest battle of our lifetime was going on, just out of arm's reach, was sheer agony for those who joined for the sole purpose of combat experience.

The AO up until Phantom Fury, generally speaking, had been annoyingly tranquil. However, during Phantom Fury, and the days surrounding both its official beginning and end, things erupted. We started taking the losses from IEDs; contact with the enemy was being made. Roaring Apaches, explosions, and fires were to be witnessed and experienced as the excitement grew. It was confirmed in this small era what generations of warfighters have expressed in their own ways: that war contains both the most extreme moments of boredom and the most extreme moments of exhilaration that there are to be known.

In mid-November, almost two years to the minute that I had graduated from boot camp, a four-man augmented team set out for a reconnaissance and surveillance mission on the Euphrates. The majority of my team proper, and the addition of Alex. Alex was former Army. One of the best operators in the battalion, but due to possessing diminished social skills in a realm undeniably familiar to my own, he rarely got credit for his universal viability.

Dez (our sniper), Alex and Chase (our automatic weapons), and I (our radio operator and OJT spotter for Dez) left our patrol base on foot. In the early morning, we found a thick patch of vegetation on the lip of the steep downhill of the riverbank. We spread out, with Alex taking the north with our biggest gun, the M240G. Dez and I overlooked the river, facing south. Chase, with his SAW, took security in an eastern direction, as it was the most open. Directly to our north, about a hundred meters away, was a blacktop road on the summit of a berm. Between the river and this berm was a field for farming, with ancient and tiny ditches running east to west.

Not really sure what to look out for, we all basically just soaked in the happenings of the morning, as the sun rose and activity increased.

Around 10:00 a.m., a gathering of cars parked behind a large area of defilade, directly across the river from our position. On our side of the river, Dez and I noticed a car, on the road behind us, pass our position three different times. We were concealed yes, but not like canopy jungle, and we hadn't dug in or built a hide. We were merely an observation post with some firepower, and we got the feeling the opposing team was well aware of our presence. In fact, this thing occurred many times to covert elements throughout the war in Iraq. Covert success was certainly achieved, but in the heavily populated farmlands on the outskirts of cities, it was almost impossible to stay hidden for long.

It was around 10:15 a.m. when we saw the canoe launch into the water. From the defilade, three men embarked northbound, toward us. Approximately three hundred meters to our east, this canoe was clipping along. We couldn't believe it; someone was actually trying to cross.

Dez and I decided quickly to call it in to our platoon commander. Waiting on orders, I zeroed in on the contents of the canoe. In time, I have forgotten about the other two men, but one I remember clear as day. He was in a black *man dress* and had shaggy black hair with a short beard. His back to me, he bent forward, awkwardly so, in a poor attempt to act like all was somehow normal. I had him in my sights. I trained on a solid space between the shoulders, following the pace of the canoe, as I waited for orders to shoot or apprehend.

Unfortunately, killer instinct did not win that day and we were ordered to physically apprehend the three. It was a source of frustration and borderline shame for many years that we were told not to blast them right out of the water.

Chase and I uprooted ourselves from the prone and began to run down the river's edge to meet them at the shore.

Immediately yelps and shouts shot from across the river. From behind the cars and vegetation a man was yelling frantically, his voice rising above all the rest. I knew something was about to happen. For just a moment I felt like gravity had lessened and blades of grass were rising to meet my eyes as my feet floated above the dirt.

The first burst of enemy gunfire erupted in my right ear. With enough timing and uniformity to impress a synchronized swimmer, Chase and I dived and rolled into a pitifully shallow ditch. To those who have experienced it, being on the receiving end of an awakened AK-47 carries with it the unforgettable and distinct *zing* of the 7.62 projectiles. The noise almost sounds like it starts with a V, and as the sound passes (long after the bullet) it turns into a whiney Z. I knew Alex and Dez were to my right, about fifty feet, and Chase was to my left at about fifteen, but I couldn't see any of them. All I could see was the lip of the tiny berm I was hiding behind, its sparse grass, and the impacts of bullets all around me. A few rounds burst into the earth so close to my face that dirt flew in my mouth.

The gunfire was not relenting. I wondered if I would know it if I got blasted in the face.

I rose up, arching my back as far as I could, exposing my head and shoulders and looking across the river. I returned fire: chaotic, un-aimed, and a full mag gone into the general area behind the defilade. There is an undeniable power that comes with efficient training. I heard myself calling out, "Changing magazines," just as I had done one hundred times before on the ranges and in the shoot-houses. It was as if someone else had jumped into my body, some classic marine seen on the old posters. I performed my combat reload and this time sighted in to take shots on whoever was spraying us with small arms fire. I really couldn't see anyone clearly, just vague shapes and hues and muzzle-flashes. It was good enough.

While Chase and I were hugging the ditch, Alex had repositioned the M240G to face the enemy, and had worked out a series of terribly ill-timed malfunctions. It was soon after I had reloaded that Alex let loose on all across the river. A full belt of ammo dropped them like flies. Those who scattered were picked off by Dez, watching from the glass of his M40 sniper rifle. Dez took three headshots, and three men fell. This lethal point-area combination allowed us to gain fire superiority, a transition whose thrill only a lucky few may know. However, despite the howling M240G and our collective concentration on the deathly bushes hiding our targets, the enemy wasn't done.

Chase was yelling. Through the noise I could make out his southern drawl, pounding out a lone syllable. I strained my ear. It became clear.

"Rose!"

"Yeah?!"

"They err shootin at us from over here!" The three who'd crossed the river had made their way to Chase's position. Hidden in thick vegetation, the three sprayed 7.62 at Chase and me.

"Are you hit?!" I yelled.

"Nah man, but—"

"Bro, your gonna have to hold 'em!"

His voice was washed over by gunfire, maybe mine, maybe his own. All I could decipher was two "fucks" and what sounded like my name again.

We were essentially in an L-shaped ambush, a dangerous and desperate place to be. On his back, rolling from left to right, literally dodging the walked-on rounds from several AKs, Chase damn near melted his SAW barrel as he took on the three.

Enemy gunfire waned for a moment, and I realized I had a radio on my back. Of all the communication training I received, and all the communications I performed in Iraq (including once relaying for my entire company during a three-platoon op, involving everything from staging a vehicle patrol base to surveillance to infiltrating multiple buildings), it was this combat sitrep[73] that I was the most proud of. Sounds easy enough: get on a radio and say what's happening, and essentially that's all it is. However, talking to my platoon sergeant and explaining in the clearest voice possible our position, multiple enemy positions, status of marines, approximate number of enemies, etc., all while being shot at…it was again the testament to efficient training to be able to execute such a thing in the manner in which it was done. And at the helm of this experience, mixed in with my frantic dissemination of any significant detail I could discern and relay, was my late platoon sergeant's voice.

"Rose, I need to know what is your current status?" he said, as calm and collected as a salesman.

A glance left, Chase wasn't motionless and covered in red. A peak to the right, the M240G smoking and crisp shots from the M40, "We're all up Gunny—but we're pinned down!"

"I understand."

---

73   Situation report

Chase's SAW roared out a volley and mixed with the M240G, engulfing me in a cacophony of sheer noise. Soon I could hear the radio again.

"Rose, I need to know their positions, we're going to try to call in air."

My mind tried to wrap around this simplest of information, yet its contents were foggy and elusive. Looking down at the green and yellow strands of grass, I muttered to myself the facts that I was piecing together. A *zing* by my head later; we are on the...north side—"Uh, we got a dozen or so on the south shore of the river, and three on the north—we are in an L-shaped Gunny, we don't have shit for cover—we're totally pinned!" My mouth was dry, and with the last globule of saliva in it, I spat out a few blades of grass that had flown onto my tongue as a lone 7.62 round exploded into the nearby ground.

"I understand," he said. His voice this time taking me to a lower stress level, albeit still a furious adrenalized pounding of the senses. My heart beat through my blouse, my armor, the attached mag pouches, and into the ground below. "Just hold what you got, we are en route."

"Roger, Gunny."

"Everyone get back to their vehicles," I heard him yell through his still-keyed handset. "Rose, I—", his voice was ripped out of my ear as my attention was averted to a new volley of enemy gunfire. My handset was flopped to the ground beside me as I reengaged a few muzzle flashes.

Firing another burst, then stopping to try to assess, I could hear Alex and Dez were both shouting at me.

"The forty is running low, dude!" Alex yelled.

"Rose, you got my ammo, man. I got two rounds left," added Dez, concealed near the only real bush in our group's proximity.

The M240G was our lifeline. Alex had gone through almost six hundred rounds, and his remaining one hundred were in my radio bag.

Admittedly, the last thing I wanted to do was expose myself again.

"Come on man, I got a liddle left! I'll cover you," Alex yelled.

So be it. There really was no choice.

On a three count, I uprooted my chest from the flattened grass and immediately heard the stew of both Alex's machine gun and the enemy rifles.

There is no way of knowing how close their rounds got to me as I ran toward Alex, prone and focused. I do know the zings fluttered in the air around me, like mosquitos, or maybe irksome tiny angels.

With a scream from the gut right out of a cliché-laden movie, I dove next to Alex and went for his ammo in my bag. My hand grabbed Dez's first, which ended up landing short of him after I hurled the bandoleer his way. Alex and I reloaded the M240G together, fast, thoughtless—right out of the training ranges of SOI. Knelt down next to the feed tray, without the time to take my own fighting position, my right ear received a deafening blast from the machine gun, so loud I could barely stand it.

It is interesting how the human mind and the human ego operate. I remember when my grandmother would fall out of her bed; she would lie and say she was doing stretching exercises. No bother the worry of why she was physically failing, it was her pride she focused on. On a battlefield in Iraq, when at any moment a hot metal projectile could rip one to shreds, reciprocity of all things demanded its relevancy. Fair was fair, and I made things right by leaning over Alex and blasting a full magazine into the enemy's concealment, making sure I was as close to his head as possible.

Distant, thundering, implosive booms came from nowhere.

"There's our boys," Alex yelled over the roar of his own ears, and with such movie bravado I couldn't help but smile. And indeed it was our boys. Looking over my right shoulder, the rest of my platoon was in our vehicles, on the road atop the berm. From the vehicles came those thunderous blasts—MK-19 grenades impacting into earth and buildings alike. The coming of our platoon, the amazing feeling, watching them laying waste to everything on the side of the river where the main threat had originated.

However, even our side of the river wasn't safe from their broad destruction. Telephone poles and wires shook, burst, and fell as hell was unleashed on that Mesopotamian shithole. Derrick was on one of our MK-19s, identified as such due to his wild blond hair that could actually be seen from our position. Upon realizing this, Dez had a minor freak-out, more terrified of Derrick's assistance than the gunfight itself. Derrick's grenades exploded all above us as the magnificent disarray decimated all that it touched.

A group got out on foot and started running toward our position; over their heads continued the crew-served weapons.

Something happened as I waited for them to link up with us. The imminent threat of death had left, and a sense of euphoria had taken its place. I scanned the south side of the river for any signs of life. There was a woman. She was dressed in a solid blue burka, and had made her way to the water's edge, bucket in hand. I put her in my sights. I rubbed my left index finger against the trigger and relaxed my breathing. I pressed against the trigger, gently. I heard a few sporadic zings from the diehard remnants across the river, hiding behind their cars. They sounded incredibly distant, though, and I watched the woman as she filled her bucket. She acted like no firefight had even taken place. It meant something to me, though I wasn't sure what, to have her in my sights. I owned her life as long as she was in them, and her next breath was dependent upon the choice of one of my fingers. She stood. No EOTech for this; I had my front site post perfectly center mass, on her back. It followed the blue garb as she began to walk back up the bank with the bucket of water on top of her head. I heard noises and the ground was pulsing. I released her from my sights, giving her back her life. I turned to see several platoon-mates halting their run to take a knee at my side.

What occurred next was a type of dubious "rescue." The truth is, it was the gun trucks that did what needed to be done. This bizarre, superfluous charge to save us was just some mad dash to see the place where the fight had already been won.

I recall someone assisting in packing my radio bag for me, and in the process kerplunked an M203[74] round into the Euphrates. Occasional blasts from the crew-serves. At some point our platoon sergeant was going apeshit. "You never fire a fifty-cal directly over friendlies' heads [indistinguishable], you dumb shit!"

Utilizing some makeshift bounding over watch, all boots on the ground made their way to their perspective vehicles. Some made it to their trucks sweating and smiling, while others were still coming off the realization that they were smack dab in the kill zone of a no-shit ambush.

Our brother platoon made its way onto the road. I could see all their faces, flaks and Kevlars a-blazing. The bigwigs had a quick powwow, probably bragging about how four guys from Triton 2 decimated the enemy at a four-to-one ratio. A little dick grabbing and maybe an "oorah" thrown out, then it was time to leave.

---

74   Single-shot forty-millimeter under-barrel grenade launcher designed to attach to a rifle

I've always wished we would have hunted the three who made it to our side of the river. Chase either killed them or scared them so badly that they were laying low.

Either way, a grenade would have sufficed.

24

LIFE OF PAIN

*When you hurt the center of your body, you know the middle back,
the lower back...there is what I like to call...a mental callous that you
have to create.*

—Phil Anselmo (a Converse x Decibel collaboration;
interview at Phil's house)

SPRING 2011

IT'S A GENETICALLY ENDOWED small frame, plain and simple.
Tiny wrists and tiny ankles. A notorious ex-girlfriend once
commented I looked better in her skirt than she did. Yeah,
I put it on, more to make her laugh, damn sure not to make
her jealous or feel "stout." Recalling that event, I am forced to see
a few haunting similarities to one of my family's most intriguing
secrets. Eventually uprooted as the awkward explosion of
repressed and tortured homosexuality, my maternal grandfather,
passer-on of said birdy frame, used to periodically whirl about in
dresses, drunk and with reckless abandon.

A disposition toward certain behavior makes pain inevitable.
A track record of fights and daredevil stunts as a youngster later to
morph into headfirst sprints into every dangerous occupation that
grinned open its rust-covered and jagged entrance.

Rolling over the hood of a car at fifteen, a plump-faced woman
was left mortified outside her town car as I picked up my bike and

rode off. On the way home I felt spider webs dangling off me. Not long after that came the blast to the spine by brilliantly jumping out of a swaying tree into murky water that hid a shallow bottom.

By sixteen, although still in possession of the graceful limberness of youth, I was a physical mess. I fought the pain, losing every time. In moments of particular frustration my reaction was to violently thrash my head about, making things worse, willingly. Doctors couldn't stop the pain, nor could my mother's Jesus.

Then...after eons...after hitting what drunks and druggies call the great "rock bottom," the inversion occurred. Finally conceding to the ever presence of pain, eyes opened for the first time. Pain became a virtue. Feeling such, being the captor of it, and defeating its tug and nag; the discomfort pulls a grin and the torture pulls you to greatness. This was found in its purest form inside a gym. Fighting fire with fire, the positive, all-nurturing, all-knowing pain swallowed whole the bad pain, which sat on a shoulder, anorexic and blackened with death.

Given enough time with the weights, and countless hours of solitary refinement, muscle has no choice but to cling to reluctant bone. Pain had meshed with discipline, as torture had interwoven with regeneration.

As much as it makes me chuckle, there are some who've accused me of being successful before. Making it to Cool Guy status in the Corps, being a usual trinket. But my money is also on because those in the inner circles never saw me fulfill the concern of shooting myself, or drowning in my own puke, in a dress maybe.

Be that as it may, whatever silver linings may exist, the origin is undisputedly traced back to a single realization. Despite all the hang-ups and maniacal confusion, I was able to notice most people loved their comfort, almost over anything else. I also noticed how dismal and mediocre these people's existence was. And this is not the judgment of someone on the mountain top—far from it. Rather it's from someone in the trenches, listening to the regrets of the common, and of their own volition.

And the cries came in: furthering education is too boring, too expensive, or too hard. Training the body is too painful, too repetitious, or it's just too much for the fit and sexy people to see you in your weak awkwardness. Moving away from friends and family is too scary, too lonely...

Well—the highbrow gadfly demands the floor—education begets both intellectual and financial wealth. The former a fixture, the latter not-so-fixed. The rigors of fitness improve quality of life: caliber of mate(s), longevity, and overall health of the mental, physical, and all the places they intersect. And striking out into the Uncomfortable is what got us out of the caves—expansion of perspective and networks enhances perceptions of life and the world as a whole. In short, the barnacle attachment to comfort neuters and dulls. It's a fluffy cage, one a succumbed underachiever can mill about in, telling their progeny that they can do and be anything, all the while, unknowingly perhaps, confirming that some people cannot.

I was fortunate enough to connect the two, the cause and effect that bogged down the faces and silhouettes of my upbringing. Without being aware of the finer mechanics, or even knowing what I was doing really, I plunged into one uncomfortable situation after the next, each time pushing the walls out just a little bit more.

At some point, as one comes up for air in the austere environments that have become something like home, one finds themselves a forger, a pioneer. The frontiers may differ, but those who dare to cut a swath are virtually free in the niches they carved.

Pushing beyond limits allowed a skinny, punk-rockish loner to keep up with some of the most incredible specimens to ever complement the ranks. You are bound to pay for it later, but when you push it as far as some have, the pain is well worth the reward, and you don't care about the scars you leave behind.

Looking at the visible ones, most from experiences only indirectly connected to my seasons as a warrior, I do an inventory of all those on my dominant side. Inches away from the scar earned from breaking that car window and pulling out the old folks is a nasty little reminder of the night I literally single-handedly destroyed some frat boys' apartment windows with a clenched fist. The drunken act amused my rather dapper and clean-cut former team leader, who soon excitedly assumed the role of getaway driver, and it was when we arrived moments later at a nearby gas station to declare I had been wounded in a knife fight that he opened up in a bellow of mirth. The mortified attendant scrounged for the right box of Band-Aids while I stole the nearest beer. Moving down is a massive gash received from an odd and blurry night where I insisted on being blood brothers with a heavy-handed friend. Further down is a token of intoxicated and dark mania, and on the top of my foot is a nickel-sized scar from the ceremonious burning of the banner at the infamous Recon River Party, which to this day was one of the greatest weekends of my life.

However, many can't be seen, and living with all the wreckage; exponentially magnified by giving flesh and bone to the Armed Way—the spinal trauma, and so forth—when done for so long one forgets it's those very things that cause so much. A glutton for punishment, yes, referred to by a police sergeant as a "masochist," that too; making the body pay, addicted. Even so, there is just no denying the uplifting elation that comes with pills and booze. Momentarily, there is a cease-fire, no need to get up and face the day. Guard down, I get to feel what others feel. I'm not constantly under the weight of living with injury, and get to experience life without the great and ever-present struggle.

There is a terrifying feeling the moment one realizes…it's never going to end. It's only going to get worse, and it doesn't care about how well you've managed so far. The truth is this is not limited to the physical nature of the body. The emotional ups and downs, often wrought from the damaged flesh, are no less real and far more potent.

I wager the serious athlete and certain types of performer can sympathize, living roughly in the same dimension in one distinct way: the body taken to great heights brings potentially some monstrous lows, and this is equally applicable to the soul as it is to the joints.

If you intend to manipulate, to show, to impress, you may experience mild suffering and pleasant triumphs. If you intend to follow the truth you feel in yourself—to follow your common sense, and force your will to serve you in the quest for discipline and simplicity—you will subject yourself to profound despair, loneliness, and constant self-doubt. And if you preserve, the Theatre, which you are learning to serve, will grace you, now and then, with the greatest exhilaration it is possible to know.

—David Mamet, *True and False*

Iliotibial band syndrome: feeling as if something bites the side of the knee. Daggers going straight down the spaces between the collar bones and the trap muscle: a type of stately execution in the ancient world. Nerves so shot that renewed electric spider webs spindle down the arms, maybe ending between the knuckles with a burning throb. Bad memories, boredom, shame, what could have been done better, those awful things they heard you say…

leaving you in the barracks to your slow-spinning fan, punk rock, and your sweat, and wondering where it all went so wrong.

I thought all the physical conditioning would somehow save me from the lying, the apathy, and the betrayals. I foolishly refined my physical nature to that of the warrior, all the while neglecting the soft things that make life truly worth living. I paid no heed to the need in me to connect with my fellow man; he was just an obstacle on the way to the gym, and later hogging the only incline bench. I was blind to the ossified state. I made myself a machine meant to handle the USMC and combat, and boy did it. USMC and combat were the easy parts. It was when this "machine" returned home...a snow blower in the middle of the fucking desert. The reverse crash, the realization of Obsolete was enough to end a man, and something to that effect must have been going on with too many distant brothers-in-arms.

Becoming so hard you callous yourself to a point of disadvantage: this is when the family really starts to worry. A caricature, a pleasant mask; bullets may bounce off, and that does a mighty service when hell is at the front door, but it does no good when the same man later can't feel the kisses going up his neck. The body armor grows tentacles, penetrating into the pink flesh underneath, imprisoning the wearer in a terrible insensitivity.

Thirty-one years old, lying in a bed alone. A quiet, empty house, more a mother-in-law suite. The light from an adjoined laundry room peeking through the crack of a deliberately open door, a white trash night-light. Terrified of the dark for some reason. Clutching a club from Africa. Waiting for something to burst through the bedroom door.

Delirium of the wandering man. I wonder how many demons pace about my room as I sleep, and there is nobody dead whom I miss.

ON THE COFFEE TABLE lay a copy of *Hunting the Jackal*, as well as *Green Eyes, Black Rifles*. An M4 with EOTech, pop-up rear sights, Picatinny rail, and twenty-nine 5.56 rounds (acquired from the Marine Corps) in an inserted magazine rests nearby against the wall. Outside the window, the pitter-patter of a summer rainstorm pelts the glass. I'm surrounded by gear and literature, a member of a great culture, yet there is discord. The demon worm burrows deep and coils fiercely inside my skull. My skills, my fortitude, owed a piece of their existence to this intruder. So inseparable from its host, the doings of such were partial extensions of this terrible thing.

I smell like the swamp, having recently returned from the rot and the fierce squirming of life underneath it. Standing against the window in a lean, forehead on my forearm, the rain burgeoning into an anticipated blanket of wetness.

I wanted to be a tier-one asset. Yeah, that was it; once I learned what the hell it was. I wanted to be the absolute best. Who doesn't? Devote myself to warriorhood as those do to the clergy. I wanted to be battle-hardened and wise, oiled and elite, a true practitioner and one to be relied on in more hairy situations than can be counted.

Feeling the mocking aches, the world granted me a different fate; and all one can do is concede how many others got it way worse.

I would fight many battles, yes, but too often from within. And unlike the reputation of the groups I would love to have climbed to, I wouldn't always win.

25

BELLEAU WOOD

We have Americans opposite us who are terribly reckless fellows.

—German private, referring to US Marines during WWI

WINTER 2012

I LIED ON MY visa. The United Kingdom wanted to know if I had any court cases pending or any charges to my name that could be treated by the British with a prison sentence of one year or more. I lied. At the time my visa application was mailed to me, I was but a mere two weeks from needing to be in London for student registration, and only one week from a plea deal in a Florida courtroom. By some happenstance, likely some unknowable technicality, or a UK passport screener as lazy as American government desk workers, pending charges were not detected and I was cleared hot. Passing one another, narrowly, like two tumbling asteroids, my application was approved just four days before multiple felony convictions were hung on my shoulders. They weren't important. I had already come to accept some colorful new titles associated with my name: armed burglar and a plethora of other nastiness that redefined the word *draconian*, along with the crusading legal practices that ensured such a black cloud. Sure, the sociological mechanism of people-titling was to arc weld a scarlet letter on me: I was never going to work for the government again, and a mere three-dollar records search would likely send a number of potential future girlfriends screaming for the hills. But I really didn't care, as surprising as it may seem. I was soon to be undertaking one of the most highly regarded philosophy programs on the entire planet. I was unshackled, and on a transatlantic flight before the ink had dried on my administrative probation letter.

Postgraduate study commenced and swallowed me whole. At the five-week mark, I was grateful that a recon buddy had come to stay with me. Having planned this for some time, it was still hard to grasp the arrival. Standing in soggy clothing, dripping rain, and wielding a lone black suitcase, Derrick stood in the lobby of my student housing. The usual swarm of students broke around him the way a river current does around a protruding log. Iraq, Camp Lejeune, Miami…some time passes and then, lo and behold, we're ready to kick it in London. Seeing one another, he smiled through the scruff, and I knew something big had just begun.

For three weeks Derrick lived with me in Bankside House, a brown, eight-story rectangle just south of the Tate Modern. His stay, a smuggling of sorts, was a true feat considering the British love for fire drills and accountability checks—lingering, I presume, from procedures of the WWII days. In this student housing, a bottom-level cafeteria worker would demand to see student IDs. Students' doors would fly open as elect wardens would make bloody sure no one was ignoring the fire alarms, ears shielded with headphones, studying merrily on their bed.

For fire drills one of us would hide under the bed, the other in the shower. More than once the door swung open, and a childish sense of rebellion surged as the door soon closed, room empty and us unfound. During the days I would head off to class, I would give Derrick my room key, coordinating the evening linkup before leaving.

Making good with one of the front door clerks served as a bypass for the overzealous security, a small group of African immigrants who were duped into thinking they were guarding the queen's jewels.

The system was probed for its gaps, the gaps were utilized, and we must have set some sort of Squatters record in that place. And as the Michaelmas term ended, we launched off the pad toward continental Europe.

Fully equipped, we had train tickets, water-resistant clothing, multiple hard copies of hostel receipts, condoms, painkillers from Spain, one working cell phone, and a marine "piss cutter"[75] to place on random statues and monuments at opportune photo ops. We were to soak in the history, food, and architecture as if by osmosis. Not in the fashion typical of the American or Japanese tourist, floating from one attraction to the next, stopping for twenty seconds to take an iPad snapshot of Stonehenge, then spending twenty minutes glamming it up for Facebook and Instagram, happy only once the perfect hashtag is plugged in. #oldrocks_rock!

Nay, we stalked and slithered every nook and addled cove. We walked until our feet reminded us of some late-night troop movement, and we ate and drank all that we could handle.

Our first stop, of course, was Amsterdam. Our hostel was without question the cheapest and most seedy lodging in all of Christendom. My snoring irritated our squad bay full of Scottish ne'er-do-wells, Australian girls with inflamed cold sores, and a German dreadlock-adorned hippy who would get up at 3:00 a.m. every night to Dumpster dive. My phone was stolen the first night, my SureFire the second.

It was a trip, no doubt, to stumble out of a bordello and see mounted police, give them a nod and then light up some hash, all

---

75   A part of formal military attire; foldable military cap with straight sides and a creased or hollow crown sloping to the back, where it is parted

the while technically on felony probation. After five days of coffee shops, museums, canal tours, window girls, window girls, coffee shops, and window girls, we said goodbye to the greatest city on earth, and its window girls.

We went to Paris from Amsterdam, by train, with blisters on our feet from walking the brick alleys and canal frontage roads of the Red Light District.

Coming out of a tube station and beholding the Eiffel Tower for the first time is no less awe-inspiring than it is made out to be. Sifting through the street peddlers, selling miniature statues of the most magnificent phallic monument in all human history, we made our way to the tower, the Arc de Triomphe, Notre Dame de Paris, and the Louvre. It was right before Christmas and the city was draped with energy and decoration.

While it is true that the Decadent movement swelled and proliferated in France, Paris is, by modern standards, not known for the same hedonistic provision that Amsterdam is. This, however, did not stop Derrick and me from sniffing out and uprooting what underworld the city had to offer.

We managed to get booted from bars two nights in a row. One night was in the Moroccan Quarter, a small corner pub with Middle Eastern squat-and-hover floor toilets. I hadn't seen one since my last time in Dubai. The patrons and bartender all could have passed as citizens from there, and one of us, I can't remember who, by a certain drink, had an amazing idea. After telling the bartender I was also a Muslim, post-conversion of my father in my adolescence, we took over the digital jukebox. Hijack our planes? Well, take some Black Sabbath, Hendrix, Tupac, and Creedence Clearwater Revival—or so went the drink-fueled mentality that evening.

The following night was a bit of a blur. After a full day in the Louvre, we bounced around some nearby pubs in the evening.

By night we had made our way to an industrial area. There is this lingering memory, without a previous event to connect how we got there, nor a clear post-event to connect some much needed dots. Finding a group of guys behind a barred gate, dressed in light clothing, these figures were reverse silhouettes in the bleak dankness that looked almost like a tiny prison yard. "Hey, how can we get in there?" I shouted, with an accent that probably sounded to them like an unlettered cowboy. We were ignored, and we subsequently wandered around in a staggered daze to wind up in some cellar bar from which Derrick was immediately kicked out. It was only after much tact and wheedling that I was able to convince the colossal, French-ebony bouncers that we were not drunk, but in fact still messed up from the Dramamine, as we indeed had just flown from the States. We were allowed to reenter but got kicked out for good a short time after. The committing of some unknown insubordination had put us back out onto the street. At some point we found the tube.

Returning to our hostel, after careening in the darkness with the luggage of girls who'd occupied the vacant bunks in our absence, we racked out. The next day would take us to a place I had been hearing about since I was nineteen; and as I spun in bed, the sound of a distant M1903 Springfield started to echo out from the near shores of recallable time.

———◦———

INTO THE FRENCH COUNTRYSIDE we were soon lost. Off the train and on foot, we had followed the one and only sign we found for the war memorial. We assumed we would see some larger-than-life monument, or touristy signs pointing even the dullest to their destination. This was not the case. Finding a quaint diner, we entered to ask the townspeople.

For my entire life, I had heard how sneering and rude the French are, in particular to Americans. The diner was smoky and hollow, like an American 1950s diner that had been abandoned for many years. The only remodeling was a new deep fryer and some full sheets of plywood covering a rotten wall. At the bar were several men, caricatures promoting French stereotypes to such a degree that it was like we had walked onto a film set. Of the four men in the diner, three didn't speak English and one, after careful attentiveness that visibly strained and scrunched his brow, could make out basic sentences. Despite the barrier, and after charades and exaggerated gestures of rifle firing and basically a bad war reenactment, they commenced to a low-mumbling huddle. Would we ever leave this place? The huddle broke up; one emerged with a cell phone. "Bell-Ah-Wude?" Zee French had come through! Before long the cab they had called on our behalf pulled into the parking lot and we were off.

To the World War I battle site of Belleau Wood, and to the place where, in many respects, the Marine Corps' reputation was born.

Hidden in hilly countryside, the weather above was overcast, just like every artist rendition that I had ever seen. The cab drove us along a winding, hard river. The road was thin and black and wrapped around every levy, mound, and stone outcropping. All the while we were trying to keep track of landmarks under the plausible assumption that we would not have a ride out of there that night. We passed through farm and thicket of autumn wood, and then onto hallowed ground.

While it first appeals to the eye as some ornate entrance to a golf course, complete with tasteful modernizations and perfectly aligned trees, there is a moment when, following the road, that a dark, elevated plot of land emerges. Knowing for sure we were there, our eyes opened all the wider, attempting to engulf its presentation: a manicured, massive lawn leading up to the wooded hillside, a lone building resembling a medieval keep, and numerous specks of white on the final lawn of the hill, what were sure to be graves.

Exiting the car and paying the fare, the wetness and chill of the air rested on my lips. Not a sound except an American flag, flapping and permanently at half-mast. Staring at the flag, months away, yet again, from my country—now one of its numerous criminals, I felt the odd sensation of being more American—and proud to be such—in a foreign place than ever in the efficiency-obsessed, congested madness that is the United States.

The picket line of trees leading up to the actual battleground looked odd and out of place. It may have just been the time of year, but they looked like the descendants of that tree in *Harry Potter* that whipped its thin branches about and tried to take the kids out when they were in that flying car.

We made our way to a small building that had a lone car parked next to it. The dampness of the place became palpable, slowly making its way through clothing and giving one that wet cloudy exhale. It was refreshing, neither of us minding the coolness.

Entering the information office, we were soon greeted by the curator. I half-expected some crusty American with a prosthetic leg recounting his erstwhile profession to droves of tourists. The curator stopped Derrick and me in our tracks. Her sheer physical beauty was striking: tall, leggy, and blonde, with a chiseled face of almost perfect symmetry. She had black boots up to the knee and was dressed like she had just performed in dressage. Meeting us with a blue-eyed smile and a "hello," she confirmed that the three of us were the only people there.

Derrick and I didn't talk for hours. We went our own ways, on our own individual pilgrimages, our Haj, randomly meeting at landmarks throughout the day.

On plaques spread about the place, the retelling of the bloody conflict was brought to life.

In 1918, the German army launched a sizable offensive on the western front. In the month of June, heavy fighting took place all over the area around Belleau Wood, which up until then was a hunting preserve. On June 6, marines, with heavy losses, advanced on the German stronghold within Belleau Wood. From that day until June 26, the marines fought one of the bloodiest and most chaotic battles of the entire war. It was almost heartening to learn that one element of the *Marine Corps Experience* had remained unchanged: plans got fucked and it all went awry. Amidst the splintered trees and mustard gas, fighting boiled down to squad level, then team level, and then even to individual hand-to-hand combat.

Little sectarian-style buildings were hidden on the hill. The stained-glass windows were vibrant under the thin, drab canopy. The whole area, especially the trees, seemed to contain a memory, some remnant of the struggle and incomprehensible destruction that had taken place.

Inside the buildings, clean and white, an American flag drooped, motionless, a legion of names carved into the walls.

Fairyland trails, straight out of a children's book illustrated by Garry Embleton, hung to the edges and cut stony or muddy aisles through the forest. Following the trails, going deeper into the woods, I discovered old weaponry, maintained and on display.

Man is the creature of circumstances.

—Robert Owen, *The Philanthropist*

I found Derrick at one of the artillery pieces. A few hundred yards away, unmarked graves read, *"Here rests in honored glory an American soldier known but to God."* Here I couldn't help but deliberate my own service. The irksome and unavoidable sensation of "I didn't do enough, I didn't get to do enough" pummeled me to the ground, an event that had occurred many times. Comparing the Marines, running through Germans with their bayonets after wading through fields of machine gun fire to IED blasts and the often impersonal assaults on farmers in man-dresses...the value difference is undeniable. But, returning to the standing and wiping the leaves from my knee, the lesson was finally realized: rarely does anyone fight the war they want to.

Why didn't I stay in? Because we didn't get to fight a war
And that's the god's honest truth.
But
Looking through a buddy's old pics
(I was too stupid to take many),
I see the smiles,
The boyish faces
Riding in a hijacked vehicle,
Gun barrel to the driver's head
In that great shithole
Together and alive.
We were doing something right.

Derrick and I both were connected to our marine forefathers that day, in a way that is diluted by the bumper stickers and lost on the back of shirts. There were trenches still visible, despite a hundred years of time settling on the place. There were bomb impacts still visible, some holding puddles. You could take a knee on the forest floor. Wet brown leaves and scattered clumps of grass. Observe your own body position, the kneeling, and could too easily be holding a rifle, as if one would readily appear if you could just stay there long enough. But, "long enough" would surpass the natural lifespan left in us, and it was time to go.

Descending out of the wood line and past the headstones, we reentered the information office.

"How was it?" she asked with a smile.

"Oh, it was really amazing, thanks."

"So did you get to see everything you wished to see?"

It was fortuitous she asked. One thing we had both heard about, and were unable to find, was a fountain in the area that marines would come to drink out of. Nothing short of a religious gesture, marines would sip from its water—the simultaneous action of paying respect and a halfhearted superstition to stave off, or dull, the VD, the Article 15, brutal divorce, effects of Agent Orange, getting beat by the female supply clerk at the division meritorious board, the annoying neighbor back home, traffic jams, suicide in the family, those who won't write back, high cholesterol, and the side effects of two decades of taking Motrin.

"Well, I am just finishing up. If you would like I can take the two of you. It's actually on the property of a nearby farm."

It may have been a type of carnal hangover from the Amsterdam excursion, feeling a lot like satisfaction just with the added element of depravity. It may have been the profound respect we had for her excited and encyclopedic knowledge of the Marine Corps. Or it could have been both, but whatever the cause, not a sexual thought was uttered nor a glance to guide a buddy's eyes to a fond spot on her body. Loading into her car, she took us down to a farmhouse, along the way verbally revisiting every square inch of history we had spent a day absorbing.

As one walks onto the property at a slight downhill, past a tiny mound of earth and turning a hard left, the fountain is on the inside wall of the mound. From a solid, man-made wall of stone and some type of mortar protrudes a rusty head of a bulldog, the mascot of the Marines. From its mouth flows the water, collecting in a moss-covered pool.

Stepping onto the wall of the pool, I noticed several unit coins and a bottle of champagne resting at the bottom. The curator watching our every move: a hesitation, and then one of us went for a sip, then the other, then a gulp, then another…all the while she stood silent, having seen US Marines perform the act innumerable times. It was time to go, but not before donning the piss cutter on the Bulldog.

As she gave us a ride into town, we thanked this angelic curator wholeheartedly, soon flagging down a cab and making the trek back to the bus station.

It had been dark for several hours by the time we made it back into the modernization of Paris, where another night of drinking commenced. This time mulled wine on Avenue des Champs-Élysées.

26

WHY GO AT ALL

WHY DID WE—THE eighties-born millennials—stop playing beer pong and go off to war?

The answer of course varies depending on who is asked. Immediately, three reasons pop up in my head: patriotic duty, career obligation, and the experience. I suppose there is a fourth category: to sate a blood lust. Did people go specifically for that? I am not quite sure. Grand curiosity, yes; the desire to kill an enemy, most certainly; but I think an even more brutal motivation than the mere act of killing develops only once you already have boots on the ground.

In a combat zone the rather annoying absence of death spurs an internal evolution. For so many who possess the simmering combination of an adventurous spirit and several years of being molded to take life, the "I want to kill a bad guy" slowly becomes "I need to kill a guy."

Being spared none of this transformation, I was always tightlipped during the many thanks for service. It's a funny thing to consider…the people we "defended" were actually thanking people who were more of the mindset of the men they were terrified of, and then of course that means, in a singular way, we are more like the men we were fighting than the people hugging us at the airport. It fades, at least for most of us. The rage. The thoughts of life-taking that make one salivate. The lethality dripping in disappointment. The fading process is as random as what spots in Iraq were hot and what spots were dead cold. It leaves some as they board the Maine-bound plane, some a decade later, some at an internal investigations tribunal for excessive use of force that pumps the veins swollen with ice water. And for some it never fades. Their bullets find a target, themselves high on the list.

By and large, however, the average citizen assumes not all this troublesome kill-talk, but rather patriotic duty. After all, it's what fuels the memes with the term "best and brightest" punched in somewhere. There seems to be this belief that those who put on the uniform and go fight are doing this out of love for their country. At first glance it seems ludicrous to think otherwise. But feelings for a country aren't just limited to feelings about its framework, but also interactions with the people in it and the systemic liberties and restrictions—for good or for ill.

It has been my experience that patriotic duty—for God and for country—was not always the case. Many who fought from my generation did so for themselves and with nothing short of contempt for the American society they came from. Going to war was a finite window to touch the vanquished barbaric world that modern reality has so woefully blighted out.

"How many people have you killed?" The answer is: I don't have the wildest idea. The mutual engagements I participated in in Iraq were like a twenty-first-century Gettysburg only with larger weaponry, a smaller scale, and with a purpose far less clear. They shot, we shot; us generally behind vehicles and/or body armor, them behind bushes and easily penetrable walls. In the end, they stopped firing and we drove off to mix protein shakes with liquor out of mailed Listerine bottles.

But how did so many end up there, psychologically disposed prior to finding their seat in a war plane?

234   D A V I D   R O S E

SMOKE STILL LINGERED IN Manhattan's scarred, deformed skyline. The news said highly trained US personnel had touched down in Afghanistan. I was living with a friend in Imperial Beach, California.

Only a Modelo can toss from the Mexican border; our neighbors were massive Samoans and large families of first-generation Americans. From our balcony I'd sit and watch elements of the I MEF[76] train in Coronado Bay. I sat there, without a job, without even a good answer as to why my friend and I moved across the country. Ah, yes, to be in a punk band. And where better than SoCal? I must have not had the moxie of Greg Ginn or Henry Rollins, because our two-man practices died quick, and we set the guitar aside to start looking for work. Watching those marines train in the bay, I had one of those moments.

Prior to, I had spent my last year in high school missing enough days to technically have to repeat twelfth grade. However, the secret agreement I made with my mother— she would excuse my Monday absence, and I would make up for it during the other four school days—allowed me to graduate.

Why I missed so much school was simply because I hated it, why else? The people, the institution, the lowest common denominator. The only reason I did so well regarding my grades is I always took a fierce, almost psychotic pride in meeting challenges and coveting the crowning achievement wherever I found a place to put it. And eventually it was over.

---

76   Marine Expeditionary Force

Finally free from the mediocrity and bondage of school, I immediately moved out. Greyhound bus to New Orleans with career-related stops in Tennessee. It took twenty-eight hours just to get to Memphis, and between walking onto the bus and walking off, I made out with a girl who smelled like Newports, watched a fistfight, got sick as hell in Nashville, and had to fend off a vagrant from stealing my bag.

I was terrified the entire trip, with the brief oasis of kissing that girl. After all, I was eighteen and came from a house where waffles, milk, and bacon were provided every morning, a twenty-minute hot shower at night was available, and some sort of roast would always be cooking on the range. I had a mom and live-in grandmother practically competing over 1950s-era housework; it could have been a reality TV show, really. *Who will win this week and get to cook the green pepper steak?* So, despite some promising dispositions, I was nowhere as hard as I would soon grow to be. There were many scars ahead, and much to learn from all of them.

Finally in New Orleans, I did some DOT stuff and was issued my Z card. Back to Mommy's house for a few months of pacing around like a caged animal and I was off.

For six months I worked for a tugboat company all up and down the eastern seaboard. Starting in the Chesapeake Bay, we were abruptly pulled from the job right after the towers went down. The company had won a contract to assist with the cleanup. We immediately moved to the Hudson. Coming in from the south, I was more fixated on the tiny, growing green sliver of the Statue of Liberty. Everyone else in the bridge of the boat was silently looking east. Men who'd seen the towers since boyhood stood there, shaking their heads, cigarettes dangling from their grumbling mouths.

The cleanup went something like this: debris loaded by crane at ground zero to flatbed semi-trucks, the trucks drove to the west Manhattan pier, a crane unloaded the truck and placed the debris onto a barge. Once full, tugboats towed the barge to the landfill site. We did this for months, around the clock, listening to sirens and the growls of crane-hearts from up past the water's edge.

Being strikingly younger than anyone else working on the tugs, "Kid" and "Cat Boy" were my new names. My coworkers in many regards were the closest thing to modern-day pirates outside an African coast. The tattoos, criminal records, muscle mass, scars, beards, drunken brawls—you name it. I came to those boats very much a naive little boy, but I left them something quite different. I got to see shades of violence that I had never seen before, a dispute resolution system that would make an ISO 9000 organizer jump out of a window. These men also introduced me to strip clubs and the shifting politics of a dodgy bar.

"I will be right here. Right outside," said my captain once, as paternal as if he were talking to his daughter about her first attempt to tinkle like a big girl.

"Come on, baby," the Newark street walker said as she wrapped her arms around me and shut the door to my captain's S10.

These men were certainly my presenters of the world. The underbelly of the world, which by the standards of some circles—artistic or otherwise—is the world. But it wasn't all booze and broads. They would redefine the term *work ethic*, and among other things show me how to power through being hungover or seasick. On those boats, there was little room for weakness, and I'm thankful that group of crusty, quirky men took me under their wing the way they did. It prepared me for the Marine Corps, if it did nothing else.

Tug-work eventually ended for me; too young, some would say. But it wasn't that. Hardly aware of it at the time, I was trying to find something, something I couldn't name. I moved back to Florida and made money by painting houses with my cousin's crew. The job had some good times and now fond memories, but after not long at all a terrible restlessness scratched at the inside of my eyes. I wanted so much more. I wanted things to fall from the sky and burst out of the earth. I wanted things to rival the Greek epics. I felt there was so much more; yet was reminded daily that I had no idea how to obtain it. At particular lows I'd lay in the complete darkness of an attic I was living in and question whether such things even existed.

Now an angry painter, I resorted to binge drinking, extraordinarily long walks at night, and the occasional bouts of vandalism. I was a powder keg. The restlessness was excruciating, and when not panting and pacing, waiting for the Great Something to happen, black blankets of depression would warmly come over me.

So, to chase the dragon's tail, came the pilgrimage to California. As was to be expected, the same monkey was on the same back. Restless, lost, and feeling trapped, I had a dream one night that I was looking at a tombstone, and on it read "Until I Have Reached Nowhere To Go." A few tiny details later, I enlisted in the USMC.

I WANTED TO GO fight, and a piece of me wanted to die in the process. I wanted it to somehow blast down an industrial stamp of legitimacy on a life that I quite simply didn't understand. Dating, even speaking, you name it...the rule books were apparently not given to me. And it wasn't just about women, God no; it was about everything. Someone laughing in that passing car must be laughing at me. Countless hours spent staring in the mirror, trying to find that thing that was wrong. Others saw it, yet somehow it always evaded me.

So yes, I wanted the violence and death. So did others. I may have been lost, but I was a hard lost, and that was far from common. I wanted to be tested, as did others. And if I did survive, I wanted to know the things only a survivor of such chaos could know. So did the others.

At nineteen, and finally with some semblance of purpose, I didn't care if the US was fighting Canada. I was an electric socket with a hard dick and a penchant for dying, and I don't know if a better or more honest assessment of a good ground combat hopeful will ever be written.

Of course we weren't fighting Canada, we were fighting in Iraq and Afghanistan. Once I decided to join, those places became some otherworldly utopia for me. Those were the places that held my glorious gunfights in welcoming arms, the places that contained the larger-than-life experiences I was to ingest and never breathe out. I expected it to be monumental, some demarcation of enlightenment on tap.

In reality, it was no such thing. I was not spared from the world and its ways I desperately wished to escape. The enlightenment was that no such enlightenment existed. Going to combat was not the remedy for all my shortcomings, as I had hilariously and bravely thought it would be. It bore fruit. It was beneficial. It was a learning experience, but certainly not what I had hoped for.

A few gunfights, countless mortars, inopportune IEDs, an old-fashion beatdown of the occupants of an entire house, a dozen or so large-scale operations, foot and vehicle patrols that bled into the other as one odd, long dream—all had their lessons to teach.

A decade later, looking down at the rifles tattooed on my forearm, I smile. The rifles crossed and the ink already beginning to fade. Yes, there were lessons learned; lessons about the self, the friend, the enemy, and the world they all occupy.

No greater lesson can be taught, though, than that of the rifle itself.

It is somewhat ironic too, if one stops and inventories all the energy spent moving away from the boot camp jargon—all the clichés about the fanatical importance of the rifle. In the right company it almost takes on a religious, metaphysical zeal. How if in far-off years spacecraft located and flew to the center of the universe, there would be—stuck barrel down in eternal, motionless space rock—a polished M16. Yet there proved to be something real in all the bells and whistles. The cheesy hype held a nugget of rugged truth all along.

The interplay between the thing that shoots bullets and the thing that makes it so has been long expressed in a somewhat romantic tradition. Although I personally never knew a single soul who did it, tradition asks when you're issued your iron, you give it a girl's name—maybe after the one back home, or that other one, or the one that got away. It speaks accurately enough about this truth-nugget, but the saccharine, Nicholas Sparks delivery of it all misses the mark in a big way. They only get the male/female thing half-right. Sexual, okay yeah—a form of codependency even, yeah that too—but the ultimate state of the relationship isn't longing stares and kisses on the napes of necks. It is a lust. A power play. A lover's tumble where both need the other to awaken the fire within.

Make no mistake about it, the relationship of the shooter and the rifle is one of switch BDSM—or switch domination and submission to the leather-wearing stickler with an eye for exactness.

Grueling. The long hours of repetition, aching muscles, and a sore back—laden with a full combat load, swinging the barrel upward from the alert to on-target for a count innumerable—the rifle is the cruelest of mistresses. Seeing the perfection that can be attained, yet falling short, over and over again, by seconds and inches. Whilst incurring a worthwhile shooting package, getting up at sunrise and having shot a thousand rounds by lunch. Good days, bad days, a round that you can't believe you let go so carelessly and then a course of fire so keyholed that all things in the outside world dissipate as something moves in your pants.

The smack of a bullet against a steel plate, controlled pairs in the black, and transition drills—all begin to lose their luster at some point to each shooter, with reference to their own diminishing marginal utility. One must fight the urge to loathe the process of weapons cleaning, to be done...yet again. Throw in some rather annoying and patronizing range safety rules, a sunburn and a blister from a piece of hot brass that somehow wedged itself in your collar, the range and the rifle itself becomes far less sexy than a gunslinger on average would readily admit.

However, after all the brass has been police called, and the clowns have all gone to bed, the skill sets earned through concentration and pain sink all the way to the marrow. Muscle twitches with a new electricity. Vision sharpened, reaction time honed, the trained shooter is a weapon wielding weapons.

For the lucky few, those who get to execute their training into the soft flesh of their target, they experience...the switch. The rifle delivers their will out into the world. It works for them—an extension of their will, manifest into hot flying metal.

27

AMPHIBIOUS, AND SOMETHING ELSE

WINTER 2004

Little Creek, Virginia. Cold as Hell.

SLAPS FROM CAMOUFLAGE BLOUSE–LADEN arms echo and bang up in the pool's rafters. Out of the water, feet soak a pair of socks then force themselves into awaiting running shoes. A trail of water goes from the pool deck through an open door and out into the darkness of the morning.

Run Swim Runs were always great for equalizing people. Strengths and weaknesses clearly came out, and all too easily. Catching up in the water or on the land, someone in the lead at the beginning could be damn near in the back of the pack by the end.

It was so cold, your frozen, tiny, tater-tot dick rubbing against your UDT[77] shorts was torture.

The senses of satisfaction, of pride, an absolute certainty that we were harder and better than…well, everyone was at their height when the personnel on base would drive by us, in their cars with the heater on, while we flew past them cold, wet, and half-crazed. The young men pale and thin, like some spread-out herd of deer on an acid trip, were embodiments of a certain, ancient determination. A determination given impetus by the blatant fact that we wanted the work, the lifestyle, the challenge,

---

77   Underwater demolition team; tiny, punitive, khaki-type shorts

the brush with death, and the title that once given couldn't be chiseled off with a jackhammer.

———◦═◦———

THE YEAR I GOT out was a big year for MMA. Matt Hughes was reigning supreme, Chuck Liddell's KO of Renato "Babalu" Sobral I must have replayed a dozen times. I missed the old tournament-based, style-versus-style UFC. Too barbaric, too unorthodox, and occupied by men on the outskirts of an unpleasant reality, the original UFC morphed into a version more akin to professional boxing standards. Though I was reluctant at first to accept the change, slowly but surely the new version was winning me over.

Then it happened: I started to notice the gargantuan tumor in the fan base.

A generation of men growing up during the highly televised Global War on Terror, mixed with the explosion of MMA and cinematic landmarks such as *300*; an aggregate, loud-mouthed, self-inflated monster was created. Leave it to the identity-less void of American white suburbia to once again facilitate a cultural trend. In the nineties it was the drug-addiction-like consumption of gangster rap, resulting in armies of white kids who trash-canned the Airwalks, skateboards, and Our Lady Peace cassettes to come to the first day of school adorned in both the urban regalia and harsh dialect that was to only be found in the most hard and tested African American neighborhoods. After a brief settling of time, the next crop were seen with heads shaven, beards to make a Tier 1 operator and/or an Octagon veteran jealous, toe-showed and competing ferociously in races with words like *Spartan* and *Tough* sloshed in there.

It wasn't originally very fashionable, though, none of it, not in the traditional sense anyhow. What motivated many men to enlist after 9/11 wasn't the same as what motivated the masculine-identity addled to grow out their beards and don their TapouT shirts in the lingered wake of it all.

The energetically lost of Generation Y. Yet out of it emerged what I like to call *Generation Why Not*, the makeup of mavericks and warriors who congregated in places like the infantry and Special Operations elements.

This is the same generation that suffered such events as the communist regimes' takeover of public school field day. Stripping the placement ribbons and replacing them with a uniform "participatory" ribbon, things like first and second place had disappeared into the wind, and trailing not far behind was their significance.

Merging back into the swarm of participatory ribbon-wearers is a violent and nauseous act, a perceived retrograde, yet necessary. With it comes some rather interesting encounters.

Orlando, Florida. A decade later. Hot and humid. At a rooftop bar.

When these kids touch our hands, they have no idea the conduction that takes place. It is my hand tonight. She is but one. Found her in an art class.

You beautiful rose, long and lean in prowess...building your body and art as one thing. Good on you, darling. Stare into my eyes. I heard them whisper about us. I saw your eyes scanning the scars and ink on my arms. Still young enough for it all to look so thrilling, yet old enough to take you to a different world...once you have peered into these types of eyes. Yes...and there you are.

What are those things? Oh, only cassette tapes. Why are you crying? It's no matter now. Ride the wind and the black to the next gruesome exhibit. Hold close, honey, I won't let these things harm you the way they did me. But? Ah yes, it is the paradox of the Wild One...these adversities have made me strong, strong enough to shield you from their very presence, and only these bad things had made me. But they have no power, below us, as we throttle past.

Looking down, she sees the addicted, loveless sex. The pointless drunkenness, the violence, both within the heart and spilled out onto faces, teeth, and the hood of a parked car.

Coming back, and coming to. She awakes, her hand in mine.

After a long pause, "You're an amazing guy." Some rain now.

She smiles faintly. Her hand retracts out of mine and is placed onto her purse. "My boyfriend is probably worried. I think I should better get going. See you in class, David."

28

THERE AND BACK AGAIN

KEY WEST HAS ALWAYS been a blast. Whether on a lone fishing trip, or with a girl, or with a rowdy group of marines, the historic and occasionally hedonistic island will never disappoint.

Bused onto the tarmac, my ARS class said goodbye to the bitterly cold intersection of Virginia's winter and spring. We were heading down to Key West to complete the Amphibious Phase of ARS, and needless to say we were not upset. The fact that our time down there was during the civilian world's spring break only heightened the high-octane aura surrounding our group as we boarded the C130[78].

Zodiacs, maps, and gradient reels. Fin time against the ocean current and lots of humidity-blanketed runs. Running twice a day dealing with the heat, sweating, and then drying off, then sweating again, to end the day by sleeping in a GP tent right out of *M.A.S.H.* Recon, the undisputed bastard children of all Spec Ops; our tent was planted in the middle of an obstacle course for Army Special Forces.

It was actually beyond enjoyable; it was in many respects the essence of masculine youth: in incredible shape, with your tribe, unaffected by the elements—alive. It was strange being in Florida with my military brothers. America's shlong was a different plane of existence, bereft of the frustrations.

---

78   Turboprop transport plane commonly used by the US military

———◦———

A MONTH LATER I would be five hours north of Key West, on leave, and for me at least, going back in brief intervals to the part of the civilian world from which I emerged, it was impossible for me not to be readjusted to one foul ass mood.

The yaw of being in a place like Camp Lejeune one day and my hometown the next was pure schizophrenia. Jumping out of helicopters into the ocean on Monday, on Thursday driving past the Dumpster at my old middle school that I would hide behind and cry, calling my mother, from a now removed payphone, begging her to drop everything and come pick me up.

A barracks party full of tattoos, sweating muscle, and promises to kill, then plummeted into a timid horde moving permanently in first gear.

If I didn't head back to Camp Lejeune after four or five days, misanthropy would start to wall me in: brick by cold analytic brick. After a week I saw roaches with Social Security numbers. The worst at the time were the proud new breeders.

They'd reach the ripe ole age of twenty-three and conclude that all the parties, trivial sex, and beach weekends were the pinnacle of single adulthood. They worked so valiantly to grow up fast, jettison from the parental nest, and experience the world. And indeed they did; but their world was only cheap, superficial feed, slopped into the trough from the same sociological powerhouses that dictated them still.

They'd have children too early, rack up excessive and unnecessary debt, then want to bay about the system somehow being slated against them. Well, they were partly right, but for the wrong reasons.

A decade or more later, however, the observations chalked up originally as developmental angst haven't blown away. The families and the debt and the excuses are all still there. Maybe in the aggressive, jungle-vine logic that gave them no quarter there'd always been some cold, hard truth.

I watch too many bloated, pathetic families, resembling some slow-moving herd of beast, or a robust bottom-feeding fish colony, limping from place to place. Mothers, grandmothers—a matriarchal elephant herd of sexless Americana, and pitiful only second to their men.

Having jammed a square peg in a round hole on the atomic level, the subjugated, pot-gut male drifts at the back of the pack.

A night of heavy drinking, years after getting out, stubble on the chin having tortured every lip on the nameless woman asleep in my bed, "tortured genius" is vomited; a necessary pressure release valve. Written on loose pieces of paper, the crumpling suggests they were likely grabbed as if trying to run away like filthy little animals. As an aggregate, the words somehow tell a story:

A pair of trousers and a wrinkled, collared shirt draped over a bamboo divider, speaking; certainly plotting my death.

The kingdom of cowards in the land of lies. Shielded by their excuses, I just have no time for them.

Can my grandmother watch me masturbate from heaven?

Fuck it, throw a poncho liner over it and bust out the spaghetti MRE's main meal.

If one had the choice to determine if the Judeo-Christian afterlife did or did not exist, what would actually be the most Christ-like answer? Wouldn't the ultimate form of metaphysical altruism be to willingly forgo your heavenly reward if it would relieve the millions who are confined to hell?

An orgasm brings suicide to mind; how the two got crossed I will never know.

When I am in a crowd I often, suddenly, daydream about being in a gunfight. Cutting the pie, buttstock firmly in the left shoulder pocket, elbows in, and feet moving the upper body like a turret. Relaxed, purposeful trigger pulls and blasts of fire from the barrel as people dive, run, and hide. Not from me. This vision existed long before actually being in a battle. Prior to, this fantasy was a rung to be reached, the true north. After the battles and the eventual return to the world of placidity, this same vision took on a new feeling. Sadly, it is gone, the days of such, less some vigilante extremism. Yet, at the same time, some feeling of realism permeates from a highly fictitious mental image. It was once the thought of a thing I was going to do in the future and now it is something behind me yet just as powerful, maybe more so. If I was stirred by the taste of blood and sand in my dreams, it was because at twenty-one we are all so suddenly pierced by the idea of the life that has yet to arrive.

Hungover, I walk past your flag, a seed in me that never really grew. A country song, a letter from a schoolteacher, and a man with a dime-sized plastic flag on his coat lapel all proclaim who we are and why we did what we did. I came from grandfathers who occasionally wore dresses and hacked their daughter's doors with fire axes: carnies, and the socioeconomic rung on our warped ladder that has no real education, no retirement. I came from the pharmaceutical dominion over the directionless. I didn't come from the America on TV; I came from the people living vicariously through the cliché and overdrawn characters in it. I didn't come from the America on the magazine covers; I came from the Walmart checkout line that gawks at them. From the living room full of secondhand smoke, I am the true American son...your true American son.

29

THE TWENTY-FIRST CENTURY AND THE TWENTY-FIRST-CENTURY VETERAN

Not a doctor—
Kill
Not a lawyer—
Kill
But a warrior—
Kill

—Marine running cadence

THE AMERICAN WARRIOR CULTURE has come home to a society that is continuously further removed from ideals and principles in which the warrior culture itself exists.

The World War II generation was participatory in the war, whether they liked it or not. Women and young people put in long, grueling hours in factories and steel mills, etc. Of course, this wasn't the case for everyone. It is arguable that the global threat during WWII was larger than those that followed, as was the war. Be that as it may, during every war since then, society has grown further disconnected from the actual blood-spilling. A blurb here, a bumper sticker there, one more deranged vet killing someone famous; Americana belly-crawls past the static to the strip mall.

There's a professed need in modern society that perpetuates preposterous entitlement, rounded edges, and a doing away with all that could harm the mind, body, and soul. Where now emotional discomfort is equal to material injury. The warrior class is without doubt embedded in a foreign land.

It is this polarity—the twenty-nine-year-old who can't point to Afghanistan on a map, next to the twenty-nine-year-old who lost a gallon of blood there—this massive societal disconnect leads to a powerful perception: one of displacement and anomie. Said perceptions are only heightened from the whispered, collective pity our own country has for us.

The pity for the GWOT veteran stems from the idea that the wars in Iraq and Afghanistan were a lost cause. And while the rest of the country knew it, we were duped, fooled, or just too damn stupid to see how blatantly futile the effort really was. Our most gallant energy and all our forged brotherhoods that we wear on our chest like some big badge of honor ultimately were done within the confines of a fool's errand, known to all but the sad uniforms carrying it to its sad end. Now technically over, but the bloodshed still raging on, we stand empty-handed as the war, our War, proved to be in vain.

The joke is on them, though. We knew the wars weren't about liberating local nationals, or any of the other post-facto dribble. We knew everything that they knew. But we also saw the one opportunity to pursue the life, packed in the facade of patriotism, that the civilized world strangles out. To see the sharpening of our iron, the flourishing of the self; and done so in the most chaotic event humanity has to offer—an armed conflict.

It's not that we are some generation of amoral existentialists, nihilists, or what have you. A common theme I noticed was the powerful admiration of the WWII fighters, and sheer envy of their circumstantial placement in space and time. It's not that we were incapable of being warmhearted liberators; we could have been, and certainly some rabidly argue we were.

But the truth is the world has changed immensely since the 1940s, as have America's enemies as well as the complexity of global politics.

All generations of warriors possess a universal energy, the common thread that connects the rifleman in Ramadi to the takers of San Juan Hill. This energy lives and breathes in the fighters of the GWOT. Souls who preferred placing this energy in a great task, a war that history may label futile, rather than no task or war at all. And the wars came.

But a real struggle hit the GWOT, damn sure as powerful as any armed conflict. In a society that relentlessly praises homogeny, the self-proclaimed color-blind, the tight-lipped, the PC-rattled—so far gone and struggling for any real identity, the transition back to the "normal life" is extraordinarily difficult. The difficulty only intensifies when one realizes how much the world has changed in only a few short years. Retrograding from a leadership role on a mobile security detail, or a platoon sergeant in a tight-knit SOF outfit, back to the rank and file, and stripped of a powerful identity the moment the plane lands—a sense of alienation and loss is likely a common occurrence. And then, of course, the hot-button topic of our era...PTSD[79].

PTSD: the diagnosis is the new black; so fashionable and accepted year round. The amazing detail in all of this (if there is one) is that it's not so much from the blood stains, bullets, air ripped from IED blasts, or the daily threat of death...but from the deafening isolation one feels when returning to their homeland, now a strange place, alien even. The distant battlefield assumes

---

79   Post-traumatic stress disorder

an awkward and unshakable familiarity. Tattoo it on the well-wishing foreheads—it is the coming back that is the trauma.

The GWOT warfighter—tested in the deserts, villages, valleys, and mountains—emerged from a nation so patriotic that it borders on ethnocentric at the very minimum. With certain, strategically placed, hyper-masculine social norms, the last lingering taste of the World War II nostalgia in our upbringing, with a plethora of violence on TV and video games, yet in a society that is increasingly egalitarian and forcibly politically correct. The lukewarm, pacified society simultaneously engineered some of the best war fighters in all of human history; what reasonable place is there for these warrior souls? At a very minimum they found an outlet for the time being, a call to action to sate their dispositions in a world that unfortunately no longer needs cave bears slain.

The warrior mentality is good to serve a purpose; however, once the purpose no longer pulls at the lapels, there is little to no place for the warrior to go. A war ending is fine for those who look at the military as a job, nothing more, or for those whose connection to the war effort results in their belief of an accomplished mission. However, those who went to war for war's sake are thus left in a terrible predicament.

It is often attributed that those who get out of the military do so due to the harsh nature of the institution, and for some that is certainly true. However, there are others, myself and many brothers included, who got out for much different reasons. The political push-pull factors, the bleeding through of the US mass-pussification into the military command structure, the sheer warmhearted blunder of full integration of females into ground combat units…they all fuse to damage what to many was the Last Bastion or, as Hemingway once referred to Africa—"the last great continent"—and without it, these many have a hard time finding where to go after. And that is it…where were we to go? There seems to be one place, at least…

The VA.

The VA, any VA across the country that is, is bursting at the seams. Parking lots overflowing, vehicles excessively draped in stickers and flags, stacked upon one another. Canes, walkers, wheelchairs, and baseball caps with ships and ribbons on them clog every entrance and exit. Relatively new to this bent Norman Rockwell painting are the droves of GWOT veterans; digital camouflage pants, beards, and thousand-yard stares wedging between men their grandfathers' age.

SOMETHING INTERESTING IS OCCURRING in the US veteran community, and politicians are noticing. Standing above all else is the relationship the federal government, through the VA, has with the veteran. The whole thing systematically crosses party lines. "Public purpose" and entitlement programs since the New Deal era have been traditionally Democrat, while pro-military hawk sentiment has been overwhelmingly associated with the Republican Party.

At certain times of the year, all one has to do is turn on any news station to watch senators and TV personalities adorn the veteran in, often, hollow praise. "Come to our side, you legless crazed fucks," as parties gear up. Disparaging a veteran is nothing short of political suicide; the veteran class is practically invulnerable to ridicule. Problem with the VA? Fix it. Disagree with the wars? Still thank the veterans—the canned "thank you for your service" will do just fine, with a free meal.

Via a few long-lasting entitlement programs, men swearing up and down to be diehard Conservative Republicans, align much harder with the current ethos of the Democratic Party than they would ever wish to know. Is the Red losing its grip on the veteran steering wheel, or is the Blue going to receive a revision toward individualism, essentially serving as a blockage toward future egalitarian agenda?

Ah, yes—the transgressive era set alive in the boys of the GWOT. Bored bad boys who'd do just about anything. They had their wars, so be it—it will have to suffice. The ideological enemy still exists and proliferates, but they had their kicks, time to move on to something else.

And just maybe, in shaping both America and the world, although pickings have taken a contemporary turn to desperately slim—through the sacred instrument of the vote—the precious idea a few of them actually thought they bled for—the veterans of Iraq and Afghanistan will be more pivotal postwar than during the wars themselves.

30

This is the terror: to have emerged from nothing, to have a name,
consciousness of self, deep inner feelings,
an excruciating inner
yearning for life and self-expression—and with all this,
yet to die.

—Ernest Becker, *The Denial of Death*

I am one time, I am right here
I am what's left, I am right now!

—Henry Rollins, from the song
"Burned Beyond Recognition"

A HANDFUL OF MONTHS after donning the ruck for the first time, the ARS student stands with an assortment of tightly packed clutter and one neatly placed sandbag inside his Alice pack. For me, it started in Camp Pendleton, where our drill instructors would take us on brief, lightning-paced speed marches. This was, come to find out later, to condition our legs for the Crucible, in which numerous hills would be summited in haste. Later, to do more of the same during Marine Combat Training. It was only when I had gotten to RIP that I was exposed to the *ruck run*, a galaxy different from the *ruck march*. Whereas a ruck march existed upon a uniform pace, meant to facilitate troop movement, a ruck run was a chaotic physical training event meant to do two things, and two things only: weed out the weak, and simulate the deep strength necessary to conduct the infamous E&E.

The Alice pack: an OD green combat backpack with metal frame, numerous small pouches, and one large main compartment. Just looking at one pokes the brain with a punji stick: a silent foot patrol in Vietnam about to get hairy. I had seen, on numerous occasions, the nasty spills bearers of a loaded Alice pack would suffer. Poor footing, a loose rock, some slippery California clay or something, all to result in a destructive and brutal tumble down a hill face. This piece of gear, like any piece of gear to be worn so much, demanded to be listened to. Adjustments become a habit, and at some point they slow down, and suddenly you are...ready.

By the time I was in ARS, I was very different than a year or two years prior. I owned the strange calluses that develop on the lower back due to the bottom portion of the frame, and trap-muscles so tight that upon the shoulder straps bearing down a .22 may bounce off, all from becoming accustomed to the ruck, and the world of the infantry in which does not exist without it.

The ruck runs would always start in the darkness. Freezing. Cold. Before the sun was even purpling the horizon, in the Virginia winter, standing in a formation, as the wind licked its way around our legs. Every student had a green ChemLight attached to the back of their ruck. The physical specimen of an instructor, soon to be leading the run, known then as the *Rabbit*, had a lone red one on his.

It started the same, always. What was a formation just a moment earlier, was now a bunch of savages exerting fiercely for their position. Some quick steps, a light jog...then into the weight-laden run, turning hard right. Down a draw made by two dunes, into sand so soft and sugary that boots were sinking instantly up past the ankle. Not even a run, but a struggle to free oneself from the grabbing sand, bursting out onto the beach of Chesapeake Bay. Forging ahead. Despite the howl of the wind, the predawn slush of the waves, followed by their retrograde, slipping into the ear. The faint whitecaps to our right, as the wind hurls featherings of sand against our faces and chests. The world has yet to come fully alive, as if operating in some dream land, on some fine border where the world we live in has overlapped by a sliver with a doppelganger world, just devoid of the Great Human Distraction. Now, with all the room one could ask for, the array of green lights jingling becomes a stretched-out body, reminiscent of some bioluminescent sea creature. Now a full run—not the sprint one would produce if only pushing his own body weight, but the shortened-step run, punishing the ground below. The wind screams in the ears, and the cold fills the lungs.

A heuristic develops, as per the runner. Some trying to stay with the Rabbit the whole time; others taking the tough terrain easy and making up the distance on the straightaways. Whatever working rule applies, it finds its groove momentarily on the beach, and is to be changed soon after…ChemLights far up ahead getting closer as they bounce, and suddenly the hard left under some boardwalk and toward the front gate of the Fort.

The sand loses its moist, packed consistency and returns to something similar to that hellish tunnel prior to the beach. The formation completely ripped apart, the student-body now a comet, a core group of animals right behind the Rabbit, and the rest at certain points within the tail, jockeying to catch the bastard in front of them; and would rather die before the footsteps heard to their rear should overtake them.

A brief run through some empty parking lot and then onto a sandy, pine-needle trail. The property-line fence to the right and a black mass of forest and fens to the left, the trail littered by the bouncing, glowing green echoes, sporadic grunts, and explosive, out-from-nowhere auditory bursts of self-motivation. All the world sucks into the walls of the trail. The eyes see nothing more, save an occasional flash of lingering moonlight on a nearby runner's pack.

The trail seems to go on forever, asking only that you lose your mind before stepping off. At some point, feeling as if that exact exchange is about to occur, emergence into a vast open area—a thin, blacktop road winding excessively through it. The red ChemLight of the Rabbit is smiling and now seen ascending the face of Loch Ness.

Loch Ness, the nickname of the steepest hill within the confines of the Fort, owns a thin but well-worn trail up one side, the side that is now being approached. A clogged amalgamation of green lights climb up through the thin spindly pines, stuck into the sand like Martini picks. At the base, the lone baby pine, worn smooth at about three and a half feet, from generations of Recon hopefuls using the stalk to propel themselves up the initial ascent. Here sets in the beginnings of the deep exhaustion. Physiological reactions like pissing one's pants, drooling, and yelling inanities as if in the front row of a Pentecostal Charismatic assembly have all been known to occur.

And that's when it happens...the reality born when the finite flesh is held up against the light of the infinite will. You push yourself so far that determination is no longer a gym-coach moniker, but the thick, viscous fluid draped to the side of your cheeks as you squeeze the rifle in your hands. There is no sense of time, only place; and unless breathing down the Rabbit's neck, the place is not good enough. The sound of your blood pumping howls, and the first car, some early-morning riser, is seen, headlights on a distant street. The route turns to road, then back to sandy trail, then road once more. A turn to the left, then to the right, and down a final slope to the hardball that is the final stretch. Nearing the finish line, those before you stand in the billowing wisps of body heat meeting the cool ocean air. A moment before ending the run that took nearly an hour, the ears pick up on the various boot strikes behind you, coming up the street, some distant and some near. The eastern sky now a faint morning blue, a man with a stopwatch yells out a time. Finished, and at a recuperative walk now, the totality of the morning's event hits the body like the booming of a wave against a seawall. Some may call it self-actualization, and maybe so. The men standing around you, panting and armored in a drenched uniform glittering from the snow, they know something that you know.

There are few places like this. A place where words, conveying their perfect ideas through imperfect vessels, mean absolutely nothing; the ideas have already been realized.

———————

SOME DISTANT FORT. SOME near Camp. A young warrior comes up from a final stretch. Staring out at the yellow, and the pink, and the gray, the morning sun rises as distant gulls call and mew. The air is still cool, nipping at his skin. But it won't last long.

In a few months he will be killed, dead from a traumatic amputation at twenty-two. But on this day, the coming sweat and expansion of crisp, clean lungs turns the body into an electric heat, in motion, kinetic energy, pistons pumping.

The morning PT session coming to an end, his unit headquarters reflects the ascended sun. He knows his home, one clothed in an immense legacy. A legacy whose maintenance, for many, was, is, and will be more important than living.

As the newest members of his unit come into view, he sees them for the soft, unmolded clay that they are, just as his forefathers saw him. He can only hope that these new ones, once seasoned to hard, will hold and exude the grit to cast down the same glare upon the distant generations that will fill the ranks after them. One only has to look to human history, baying that this grit will remain, popping and gurgling over societies' edges at times opportune and inopportune alike. And if not? Something very special, and very beautiful, will have been lost.

AUTHOR'S NOTE

G ETTING THIS TO PRINT was a whiplash carnival ride of passing faces; excited friends, appalled editors saying 'no,' agents, managers, self- and vanity-publishing solicitors, swindlers, and the few beacons of light out there in all the swirl.

Thank you, David Aretha, Mike Scotti, Rob Price, and Tyson and posse at Rare Bird: islands in the stream.

Finally, thank you to numerous gunslingers, alive and dead. Of the living particular: Devin Denman and Rob Glenn. Alterations at their minimum, your memories filled the gaps that a good portion of the exploits listed undoubtedly made. Beyond the enthusiastic criticism, your humor, perspective, and chain texts nurtured the embryo of this project.

—Orlando, Florida

GLOSSARY

.50-cal/caliber: M2 machine gun; crew-served, air-cooled, belt-fed machine gun firing .50-caliber BMG cartridges

A2: Alpha Two; platoon I operated in while deployed to Iraq; there were three platoons in Alpha Company: A1, A2, A3

AO: area of operations

ARS: Amphibious Reconnaissance School; this was the East Coast school that produced Marines of the Recon MOS; there was, at the same time, a West Coast version, BRC (Basic Reconnaissance Course), that eventually was revised and made the sole school for Recon

BAH: basic allowance for housing; a significant financial and lifestyle perk, and incentive to get married while in the military; also the primary food source for the Dependapotamus

BZO: battle sight zero; adjusting sights of a weapon to obtain accuracy, as per the individual shooter

BDA: battle damage assessment

BUDS: Basic Underwater Demolition School; where Navy SEALs are born/made

C130: turboprop transport plane commonly used by the US military

CAG: Combat Applications Group, aka "Delta Force"; a tier-one asset and no you don't know anyone in it

CAS: close air support

CAX: combined arms exercise

CO: commanding officer

CONUS: within the contiguous United States

Dependapotami: plural form for Dependapotamus; a parasitic military wife, generally to the enlisted, whose ratio of labor to benefits is asymmetrical; her normal stratagem is one child per spouse's deployment or enlistment, whichever is of the greater value

E-6: staff sergeant; of the enlisted rank structure, working up from E-1 to E-9

EGA: Eagle Globe and Anchor; iconic symbol of the Marine Corps

FSSG: Force Service Support Group

GP: general purpose; large tents usually used to house numerous military personnel

Gunny: Marine shorthand for gunnery sergeant; E-7

GWOT: Global War on Terror

Hardball: slang term for paved roads

HRST: helicopter rope suspension training

ID: infantry division

IED: improvised explosive device

ITB: Infantry Training Battalion; portion of SOI designated for infantry students

KIA: killed in action

Libo: "liberty"; time off

LZ: landing zone

M203: single-shot 40 millimeter under-barrel grenade launcher designed to attach to a rifle

M240G: belt-fed, gas-operated medium machine gun that fires the 7.62×51-millimeter NATO cartridges

MCIWS: Marine Combat Instructor of Water Survival

MCMAP: Marine Corps Martial Arts Program

MCT: Marine Combat Training; portion of SOI designated for non-infantry students

MEF: Marine Expeditionary Force

MEPS: Military Entrance Processing Command

MEU: Marine Expeditionary Unit; quick-reaction force, deployed generally via ship

MILES: Multiple Integrated Laser Engagement System

MK-19: pronounced "Mark 19"; belt-fed, blowback-operated, air-cooled, crew-served, fully automatic grenade launcher

MOS: military occupation specialty; fancy term for someone's job

MP: Military Police

MRE: meal ready to eat

NVGs: night vision goggles

OCONUS: outside the contiguous United States

OD: olive drab

OIF: Operation Iraqi Freedom

OOD: officer of the day

OP: observation post

PFC: private first class; E-2

Piss cutter: part of formal military attire; foldable military cap with straight sides and a creased or hollow crown sloping to the back, where it is parted

PJ: Air Force Pararescue

POA: position of attention

POW: prisoner of war

PT: physical training

PTSD: post-traumatic stress disorder

PX: post exchange; convenient store on military bases

QRF: quick reaction force

Quadcon: large ground container used by the US military

RIP: Reconnaissance Indoctrination Platoon

ROE: rules of engagement; aside from getting servicemen killed, it theoretically functions as a framework for order and a moral code in the combat setting

RPG: rocket propelled grenade; common weapon of enemy in both Iraq and Afghanistan

SAD: Special Activities Division

SARC: Special Amphibious Reconnaissance Corpsmen

SAS: Special Air Service

SAW: M249 squad automatic weapon; belt-fed light machine gun that fires the 5.56 ×45-millimeter NATO cartridge

SERE: Survival Evasion Resistance Escape

Sitrep: situation report

SNCO: staff non-commissioned officers; E-6 to E-9

SOF: Special Operations Forces; this encompasses all Spec Ops in the US military; intent on employing and training the smartest, strongest, and toughest individuals to complete difficult missions under the harshest conditions

SOI: School of Infantry

SOP: standard operating procedure

TQ: Al Taqaddum Airbase; an airbase in central Iraq

Triton 2: see A2

UCMJ: uniform code of military justice; the authority in military law and regulation

UDT shorts: underwater demolition team; tiny, punitive, khaki-type shorts

VA: Department of Veteran Affairs

VBIED: vehicle-born improvised explosive device

XO: executive officer

Zaidon: rural area, south of the city of Fallujah, in the Al Anbar Province of Iraq